Twayne's English Authors Series

Sylvia E. Bowman, *Editor*

INDIANA UNIVERSITY

George Crabbe

 18

George Crabbe

By ROBERT L. CHAMBERLAIN

Grand Valley College

Twayne Publishers, Inc. :: New York

To BOBBI *and* TONY

Preface

This book about George Crabbe has as its first aim the introduction of its reader to the works of an English poet whom he may well never before have read, even in an anthology. But it also aims at defining and illustrating Crabbe's particular claims to greatness as a poet and at identifying, as well as can be done, his peculiar place in English literary history. I have adopted the chronological review as the approach best suited to this threefold purpose, but I have varied this approach from time to time for the temporary sake of one of these aims.

It is a changing poet I trace: the early Crabbe, a writer of original powers but hampered by Augustan modes and manners and by the rancor of disillusionment, gives way to a middle Crabbe, whose art has become surer because more independent, whose horizons have brightened and expanded, but whose opinions the times have tampered with and whose temperament is still strangely tinted by pessimism. In the *Tales in Verse* (1812) and the *Tales of the Hall* (1819), however, Crabbe comes finally into his own. And these two works have led me to support some rather large claims for Crabbe—as an original and skillful handler of the heroic couplet in a period when it is generally supposed long since to have turned effete; as one whose artistry converted events and people from real life into the plots and characters of dozens of first-rate short stories in verse and a verse novel; as one of the important figures in the history of English poetic diction and one of the more curious in the history of aesthetics; and, finally, as an artist in whose work the relationships among the raw material, their shaper, his product, and the audience are of the highest significance.

The chronological approach has encouraged my handling Crabbe's life piecemeal. Details of his life are so frequently reflected in his verse that I can only trust to have kept Crabbe the man in the background. His poems and the life of the spirit they reflect are the book's true subject—not the life of the man or the face of his times. This book contains, consequently, less than the usual critical emphasis on Crabbe the Realist, the Social Historian, and the Photographer in Verse, or on Crabbe the Ducal Chaplain, the Absentee Rector, and the Vicar of Trowbridge. Consequently, it pays more than the usual respects to Crabbe's last great work, *Tales of the Hall.*

The large majority of commentators on Crabbe classify him as an unmistakable Neoclassicist; a small but articulate minority claim him as essentially a Romantic. If I incline towards the minority's view, it is partly to help redress what seems to me a critical imbalance. But, in the last analysis, I prefer escaping the problem by disassociating Crabbe from either school. My central point in this study—if it can be simply put—is that the subject of Crabbe's poetry, poetry bound to this world and our life and to his England with hoops of steel, is as surely Everyman as it is the Reverend Crabbe or Suffolk farmers and fishermen or the bourgeoisie of Leicestershire or Wiltshire; and that this relationship is of great importance to us, his readers.

No appreciation of Crabbe, who is essentially a narrative poet, can avoid extracting rather liberally for quotation. To keep the documentation to a minimum, I do not acknowledge such quotations in the text unless they come from a source other than A. W. Ward's three-volume edition of Crabbe in the Cambridge Classics. All biographical data may be found, unless otherwise identified, in either the life by Crabbe's son (1834) or in the life by Huchon (1907). I have taken one liberty in reproducing Crabbe's poetry: I have omitted the unnecessary quotation marks with which Crabbe often began each verse of a character's speech.

The bibliography at the end of the volume excludes, for obvious reasons, references to works not in English. I should mention that it does not indicate, therefore, the surprising amount of interest shown in Crabbe on the Continent—notably in France, Germany, Holland, and Russia. Everyman is not a British citizen.

ROBERT L. CHAMBERLAIN

Grand Valley College
September, 1964

Acknowledgments

The earliest and fondest of my indebtednesses is to Howard Brogan, whose interest in Crabbe awakened mine many years ago; in the intervening time I have continued to profit much from his advice, as well as from the friendly interest and opinions of Arthur Hoffman and Arthur Sale. I must express, too, my appreciation of the various aids and kindnesses extended me by Sir John Murray, KCVO, DSO, who permitted my transcribing the many poetical manuscripts of Crabbe in his possession and lent the photograph of an oil painting of Crabbe reproduced on the dust-jacket; by the Earl of Cranbrook; and by the librarians of Syracuse University, Cambridge University, Oxford University, the British Museum, the University of Illinois, and Grand Valley State College. To the University of Illinois I am indebted besides for financial assistance in preparing the typescript of this book.

I am pleased to express gratitude to the following publishers for permission to use extracts from the works cited: Chatto and Windus, Ltd., F. R. Leavis' *Revaluation,* Lilian Haddakin's *The Poetry of Crabbe,* and Frank Whitehead's *Selections from George Crabbe;* Columbia University Press, Basil Willey's *The Seventeenth Century Background,* and H. N. Fairchild's *The Noble Savage;* Constable and Co., Ltd., W. H. Hutton's "Some Memories of Crabbe" in *Burford Papers;* Harcourt, Brace and World, Virginia' Woolf's *The Captain's Death Bed and Other Essays;* Holt, Rinehart and Winston, a translation of Hesse's *Demian;* Methuen and Co., Ltd., T. E. Welby's *Second Impressions;* the Society of Authors and Dr. John Masefield, OM, Masefield's *Recent Prose,* and the Society of Authors and the Public Trustee, G. B. Shaw's *Arms and the Man;* Oxford University Press, M. H. Abrams' *The Mirror and the Lamp;* Viking Press, Lionel Trilling's "Art and Neurosis" in *The Liberal Imagination;* and to the publishers of certain other books whose use I have acknowledged in my footnotes.

Contents

Contents

Chronology

1754 George Crabbe born December 24 in seaside village of Aldeburgh, Suffolk, eldest son of George Crabbe, local customs official and onetime parish clerk and schoolmaster.

1763- At school in Bungay and Stowmarket, both in Norfolk.
1767

1767 Employed by father as dock laborer at Slaughden Quay, just south of Aldeburgh.

1768- Apprentice to apothecaries and surgeons in two Suffolk
1775 towns; on the side, composed poetry and studied botany.

1772 In Woodbridge, Suffolk, met and began courtship of Sarah Elmy, his future wife. First poems published in two magazines.

1775 *Inebriety* published anonymously in Ipswich. Crabbe returned to Aldeburgh, worked briefly again at the quay, then set himself up as a "doctor." Continued to study literature and natural history.

1776- Spent ten months studying medicine, especially obstetrics,
1777 in London; returned to his Aldeburgh practice.

1779 First draft of *The Library*.

1780 April, abandoned Aldeburgh and his inadequate practice for London and literature. August, *The Candidate* published anonymously in London. Death of his mother.

1781 Spring, rescued from oblivion by Edmund Burke, to whom—after a year of fruitless efforts to earn a name, a patron, or a living—Crabbe had appealed in an eloquent letter (see George Crabbe's *Life*, 90-93). Burke introduced him to Fox and Reynolds (he met Johnson two winters later), got his *Library* published (in July), and had him made a deacon and appointed curate to the rector of Aldeburgh.

1782   August, ordained; removed to Belvoir Castle, Leicestershire, as chaplain to the Duke of Rutland.

1783   May, published *The Village*. December, married to Sarah Elmy after eleven-year engagement.

1784   First child born and died.

1785   March, published *The Newspaper*. Became curate at Stathern, Leicestershire. Birth of son George, his future editor and biographer.

1786   Death of his father.

1789   Received new livings in West Allington, Lincolnshire, and Muston, Leicestershire. Moved to Muston.

1792   Moved to Parham, Suffolk, to live on property inherited by his wife Sarah.

1793-   Death of two youngest sons. In 1796 Sarah began to
1796   suffer from a "nervous disorder" that increased until her death.

1795   Published "Natural History of the Vale of Belvoir" in *The History and Antiquities of the County of Leicester*.

1795-   Wrote botanical treatises, poems, novels; destroyed most.
1807   Those not destroyed which were published in 1807 *Poems* are *The Parish Register* (begun 1802, finished 1806), "The Birth of Flattery," "Reflections," "Sir Eustace Grey," "The Hall of Justice" (written 1798), "Woman."

1804   *The Borough* begun; finished 1809; published April of 1810.

1805   Required by his bishop to return to his living at Muston after thirteen years' absence.

1812   September, *Tales in Verse*.

1813   Death of Sarah, his wife. Crabbe became very ill but recovered.

1814   Removed to Trowbridge, Wiltshire, as rector. Briefly engaged to Charlotte Ridout.

1814-   Lived in Trowbridge but enjoyed visiting elsewhere—
1832   nearby Bath and distant Suffolk frequently, London occasionally (where Campbell, Moore, Rogers, Murray, Lord Holland, Southey, and even Wordsworth paid him respectful attention as the last great contemporary of "the giants before the flood"). Went to Edinburgh to visit Scott.

1816   December, his very recently married son John became

his curate at Trowbridge and moved into the rectory.

1819   July, *Tales of the Hall*, two volumes.

1822   Began to suffer from facial neuralgia. Published *The Works of the Rev. George Crabbe,* seven volumes; re-printed in 1823 in five volumes and in eight.

1822-   Composed the poems, never wholly revised, published in
1824   1834 as *Posthumous Tales*.

1832   February 3, Crabbe died.

1834   *Posthumous Tales* published.

George Crabbe

CHAPTER 1

Portents

IN his twenty-third year the unknown but very hopeful poet
George Crabbe published his first long poem, *Inebriety*
(1775). At that time Samuel Johnson, who seven years later cor-
rected in manuscript Crabbe's first important poem, *The Village*
(1783), was still presiding over English literature. When
Crabbe died in 1832, widely known and leaving behind him
a yet unfinished series of tales in verse, only Wordsworth and
Coleridge were left from among the major figures of the
Romantic movement. Between 1785 and 1807 Crabbe published
no poetry whatsoever, but during these two decades he committed to periodic bonfires (the delight of his children) a
quantity of verse, three novels and an authoritative botanical
treatise which he was discouraged from publishing because it
was not written in Latin. Nevertheless, he managed to bequeath
us approximately thirty-two thousand heroic couplets and several
thousand lines of other kinds of verse. Only a fragment of all
this work appeared in the eighteenth century, the century to
which his name has been attached.

The reader who comes to Crabbe fresh and unadvised, acquainted at most with *The Village,* can hardly know where to
begin. Bewildered by quantity and baffled by the curious
qualities of that quantity, he is likely soon to close his borrowed
volumes convinced that minister-poets writing in couplets are
simply not for our time. Some of Crabbe's contemporaries also
branded him as not for their time. Others, however, paid him
remarkable tributes. Byron, for example, paired Crabbe and
Coleridge as the greatest of living poets. Jane Austen deduced
from Crabbe's poetry—she had never met him—that Crabbe
was the only man she might consider marrying. Two years
after Crabbe's death, Wordsworth was willing to go on record
as saying that his works would "last, from their combined

merits as Poetry and Truth, full as long as any thing that has been expressed in verse since they first made their appearance."[1]

Wordsworth was too generous. In a basic sense of the word, Crabbe's work has not "lasted" at all as well as Wordsworth's own, fragments of which every high school student commits to memory. Yet Wordsworth was right in believing that it deserved to last as long, and an admirer of Crabbe has recently remarked, perhaps over-enthusiastically, that little more than a tenth of Wordsworth's output is today readable as contrasted to "close to one-fourth" of Crabbe's.[2] So different, however, is the best of these two poets' work that the reputation of Crabbe has suffered unduly from the enormous influence which Wordsworth and the movement he may be said to represent have wielded upon our literature, our criticism, and our sensibilities. Crabbe's reputation has suffered also from our confusion over his position in English literary history. We have not been able to classify him satisfactorily. Poets who escape the tags of literary movements make us uneasy; we may prefer simply to turn our backs upon them.

In the concluding decades of the eighteenth century, Crabbe was regarded as a promising new voice in the chorus of poets who, it was later to be estimated, were anticipating the Romantic outburst. In the third decade of the next century, he came to be regarded as the great but fading anachronism of the age: the poet who might still be toiling away in the Augustan mode years after the deaths of Keats, Shelley, and Byron. By the end of the nineteenth century, Crabbe was being occasionally claimed as a Victorian Realist born a century early—and among the Victorians who show distinct evidence of his influence are such unlike writers and questionable "realists" as Tennyson and Hardy. In our own times, Crabbe has been seen as born, in fact, a century and a half too early: he has been called a Modern by virtue of his recognition of the subterranean powers of sex and his accent on disillusionment and anxiety. Over all these years he has been variously labeled an Augustan, a Romantic, a Realist, and a Naturalist; a psychologist, a moralist, a scientist, and a social historian; a satirist, a tragedian, a humorist, and a photographer; a nihilist, a Calvinist, a conservative, and a progressive. And he has been likened to Dostoevski, Chaucer,

Dickens, Dryden, Juvenal, Sainte-Beuve, Balzac, Cowper, Landor, Byron, Wordsworth, Blake, Dante, Maupassant, Hesiod. But can he have been all this? Though the mind begins to titter at such listings (the possibilities have not been exhausted), they do suggest something of the ambiguity of Crabbe's achievement; and that ambiguity, in reality an index to his peculiar kind of greatness, has unfortunately helped relegate him to a grave of general neglect.

Only certain independent readers, uncommitted to the fads and fashions perpetuated by much criticism and most textbooks, have taken Crabbe seriously enough to advise his disinterment—readers like Edward Fitzgerald, John Henry Newman, Virginia Woolf, Ezra Pound, E. M. Forster, H. J. C. Grierson, and F. R. Leavis. As for the uneasy anthologists, they have too often decided to omit Crabbe altogether from their aquariums rather than set him swimming with a literary school from which his divergences might seem so ungainly. Although so undervalued for a century as to be unknown now, to most readers, Crabbe may well belong, as a recent editor has forcefully argued, among the greater English poets.[3] No cursory glance at the quaintly humdrum surface of his poetry, nor even thoughtful attention to a few excerpts can give a true indication of the range and power of Crabbe's work, especially in the realm of verse narrative. He needs to be read in quantity, and for those who wish to do so the following two lists are designed. The first list offers the quicker introduction to Crabbe's better work, but the supplementary list provides a more leisurely and therefore more representative selection.

List I: from *The Borough,* one should read "The Vicar" (letter II), "The Parish Clerk" (XIX), and "Peter Grimes" (XXII); from *Tales in Verse,* "The Parting Hour" (tale II), "The Frank Courtship" (VI), and "The Confidant" (XVI); from *Tales of the Hall,* "The Adventures of Richard" (part IV), "Delay has Danger" (XIII), "The Natural Death of Love" (XIV), and "Lady Barbara" (XVI); from the *Posthumous Tales,* "Silford Hall" (tale I) and "The Family of Love" (II); and the poem entitled "Flirtation." List II: from *The Library,* lines 535-94; from *The Village,* the first book; from *The Parish Register,* "Burials" (Part III); from *The Borough,* "General Description" (letter I), "Election's." (V), and "The Alms-house and Trustees," lines 88-339 (XIII); from *Tales in Verse* "Procrastination" (tale IV), "The Mother" (VIII), "Arabella" (IX), "The Lover's Journey" (X), and "The Brothers" (XX); from *Tales of the Hall*, "The Preceptor Husband" (part IX), "Sir Owen Dale" (XII), and "Smugglers and Poachers" (XXI); from the *Posthumous Tales*, "Master William" (tale XIX); and the poems entitled "Sir Eustace Grey," "The World of Dreams," and "Infancy—a Fragment."

Crabbe's life also needs to be read, and no summary of his apparently humdrum existence, much of it devoted to the routine of pastoral duties, can indicate the depths to which Crabbe's experience took him, or the profundity of his response to life. The better way to approach Crabbe, the man and poet, is not through random criticism nor the definitive, impressively scholarly study of his life, work, and times by René Huchon, but through the briefer, affectionate, often touching, sometimes deeply moving biography by Crabbe's son that was begun while his father was still alive and concluded soon after his death.

This minor classic, which is the first volume of the 1834 *Works* (frequently reprinted since), ought to be the most persuasive of introductions to Crabbe's poetry. Less accurate and much less detailed than Huchon's study (to which a reader might profitably turn *after* coming to know Crabbe through his poetry), it is superior for the sensitivity with which it reflects—like the poetry whose content and spirit it was meant to portend—the inner life of the poet. Honoring the misguided advice of friends of his father—Thomas Moore, Samuel Rogers, John Gibson Lockhart, and others—the son "obliterated" parts of his biography before publishing it, but the work survived the tampering and remains unmistakably honest. Where it is evasive or disappointingly silent, we continue to trust it; for we perceive the son's refusal knowingly to deceive or mislead, no matter what may be the demands of biographical decorum as defined by his father's less talented friends.

The Crabbe of this book is a sympathetic figure but not a sentimental one. It would be easy to sentimentalize Crabbe's life, for the right ingredients are there. Born in obscurity and comparative poverty in Aldeburgh, a small village on the Suffolk coast, one of England's less exotic seasides, Crabbe realized in London his adolescent dream of becoming a famous poet—realized it suddenly but only after a long, uncertain struggle, that prerequisite of sentimental triumphs. When fortune did favor him, he became "overnight" an associate of some of the most illustrious Englishmen of the day (Edmund Burke, Samuel Johnson, Sir Joshua Reynolds); married the sweetheart of his teens, Sarah Elmy; and, as chaplain to a noble family, went to live in a castle in the vale of Belvoir. So might the resumé of this happy life run on, telling of quiet decades in rural parsonages, of resounding acclaim from literary circles, of a parent's trials and a rector's pleasures—a resumé glibly absorbing such intransigent matter as the death of five of Crabbe's seven children or the insanity that began to overtake his wife in middle age and that increased yearly for the twenty years she continued to live.

Miserable as an ill-trained midwife and surgeon, his first means of livelihood, hardly more happy as an unpopular curate back in Aldeburgh or as a necessarily obsequious servant of nobility, thereafter frequently disappointed in his hopes for clerical preferment, forced to prolong his engagement to Sarah to eleven years, victimized by a painful variety of *tic douloureux* (a facial spasm) and of stomach disorders that kept him on opium nearly half his life, susceptible to guilt-ridden nightmares—Crabbe can in no simple sense of the word be said to have led a happy life. It was, rather—or therefore—a meaningful life. Both the son's biography and Crabbe's poetry impress strongly upon us things we need repeatedly to be reminded of: happiness and success can never be readily defined; should never become one's aims; and are, indeed, attainable only in forms so different from what one has conceived as to be often unrecognizable.

Crabbe's work has the reputation of being the repository of a gloom unique in English literature. The reputation has foundation, but it represents only half the truth—and it is most unfortunate that William Hazlitt's prejudiced but influential characterization of Crabbe as a versifying misanthrope morbidly gloating over a vast infirmary[4] remains better known than

Crabbe's poetry. Certain it is that Crabbe came early to a cautious view of life's possibilities. In a long extraordinary fragment of a poem entitled "Infancy," first published in 1834 but written in April of 1816,[5] Crabbe in his sixties looked back upon a particular day when, as a child, he had dimly perceived through metaphor that life's pattern was to be one of promises unrealized and of pleasure turned to pain. After arguing, rather abstractly, that pleasure is actually no more than the absence of pain, which even now, Crabbe writes, "controls me like my lawful prince," the fragment glances at several real griefs and terrors in Crabbe's childhood, then handles in detail that day when the boy Crabbe was permitted to join his elders in an excursion up the river Alde by boat:

> I heard them say
> "Let the child go; he will enjoy the day."
> For children ever feel delighted when
> They take their portion, and enjoy with men.

During that early morning sail, all seemed well; but by midday the boy, uneasy now, found himself lost in a strange riverside town. When he did manage to rejoin the adults, he discovered disturbing change: the men were becoming demoralized by drink; and the women, as a consequence, were fretful: "and, as the sun declined,/The good, found early, I no more could find . . . ." The return voyage is alarming, for the men maneuver the boat recklessly and "nervous women would be set on shore." Evening brings more than sunset chill to the river. It brings a storm. The day which had begun with joy and expectations of more joy, with birds singing in the sunlight of a world that seemed like "paradise—because within/Was a keen relish, without taint of sin," has brought with it confusion, dismay, and fear and has ended with rain, lightning, and thunder.

This, then, is that "portion" that men must "enjoy"—a portentous experience for the child Crabbe, whose plans in later years bore so often either strange fruit or none at all. His reader soon discovers that Crabbe's poetry follows the pattern of his life; Crabbe's life, he himself discovered, followed the pattern of that excursion day—with one very important difference. This difference lies in an affirmative counterforce in his life which is not reflected in "Infancy" but was being given its fullest and most moving expression in the major work he had already begun, *Tales of the Hall* (1819). Elsewhere in his poetry, this carefully leashed but irrepressible impulse towards optimism finds most frequent expression in frequent wit, some bad puns, and much good humor. It is also present in the Crabbe recreated in his son's biography.

It is almost wholly absent, however, from that first important poem, *The Village*. This is one of the reasons why our survey of Crabbe's work ought to begin with this vigorous but confused and untypical work—one so untypical as to portend very little of the Crabbe who wrote *The Borough, Tales,* and *Tales of the Hall* nearly three decades later. Apart from "Peter Grimes" (*The Borough*, XXII)—the main source of Benjamin Britten's well-known mid-twentieth-century opera of that name—*The Village* is Crabbe's only widely read poem; and because it so ill represents him, its relative popularity has done its author several disservices. For a century, most reprinters of this poetical essay have perpetuated misjudgments regarding its position in English literature, misconceptions regarding its significance in Crabbe's work, and hence misunderstanding regarding the very nature of Crabbe's accomplishment as a poet.

CHAPTER 2

Essais

I *To Sing of Shepherds*

WHEN *The Village* first appeared in May of 1783, it deserved, more than it does today, to be widely read; and so it was. Favorably reviewed in three important journals within half a year and thereafter excerpted in two popular anthologies,[1] it struck its readers as an energetic poem. It may well have seemed, as Johnson had said it was, "original, vigorous, and elegant."[2] No longer does it impress us as either very original or very elegant; but it is vigorous still—vigorous because written in sufficient anger to raise it above the several literary types it tries, rather unsuccessfully, to fuse. In some half dozen passages, its language, logic, and even movement and sound give full service to Crabbe's attack upon pastoral poetry's traditional misrepresentation of the facts of country life.

The poem really contains more of country than its title should allow. The title functions chiefly to indicate the poem's literary type and to allude ironically to the idyllic picture of rural village life presented in the first part of another member of the type, Goldsmith's *Deserted Village,* published thirteen years before. It is wrong, though, to assume that Crabbe's village poem is an answer to Goldsmith's. Crabbe's poem has neither the structure nor the consistency that a planned rebuttal would require—and the two poets actually shared some views: that contemporary village life was a sorry spectacle and that the economic gulf between the classes was dangerously widening. What Crabbe did do was make frequent use of references covert and overt, including a direct quotation, to Goldsmith's poem that had recently and rapidly won the special place in English hearts it still holds, a niche from which even Crabbe may have realized it need not be dislodged.

The allusion to Goldsmith's vision of sweet Auburn is begun in Crabbe's opening lines, whose grim point he allies to an unconventional invocation:

> The Village Life, and every care that reigns
> O'er youthful peasants and declining swains;
> What labour yields, and what, that labour past,
> Age, in its hour of languor, finds at last;
> What form the real picture of the poor,
> Demand a song—the Muse can give no more.

The muse's drastically limited role as inspirer comes as climactic anticlimax to that word "demand" and to the crescendo of the preceding word cluster—*care, youthful, declining, labour, languor, real*. The poem is to be, obviously, a corrective work and its inspiration personal experience. For that phrase "the Muse" we may read "my Muse," which is to say—for this is Crabbe's bold assumption—"Truth." The bucolic Muse, having long peopled Western literature—lyric, dramatic, epic, and narrative—with delicate shepherds and exquisite shepherdesses, had "given" many an eighteenth-century English poet material quite different from what Crabbe's muse promises. So his aim is both to tell the rough truth and to banish from literature and from man's mind those gentle-mannered, never-aging swains and nymphs whose remotest and certainly quite unlike ancestors had been a Sicilian peasantry known to Theocritus. Other Greek writers (Bion, Moschus, Longus) had transformed these peasants into almost wholly literary figures, and the transformation was continued by such Latin writers as Virgil, who settled them in the literary country Arcadia, and Horace. This happy peasantry had eventually "migrated" during the Renaissance through Italy and France into England. There their hold upon the English imagination and its literary counterparts was assured by highly influential writers—Sidney, Spenser, Shakespeare, and a dozen others up to Milton.

Even when poets did not employ the figures and motifs of pastoral convention, poets had often presented country life as something akin to life in paradise, a condition of essential innocence, its rustic serenity broken only by outbursts of elegant romantic passion or poetic fervor. If the vile, corrupting serpent ever insinuated himself there, he came not as symbol of man's corruptibility but as agent of man corrupted by city and court. All this was too much for Crabbe. Taught by experience to be wary of passions and fervors and convinced that innocence and maturity are incompatible, Crabbe knew that however unsullied might be the impulse which leads fallen man to conceive a present or future terrestrial paradise, the place must be as imaginary and therefore as dangerously misleading as the happy valleys of pastoral verse. Ever since "vice the world subdued and waters drown'd," he wrote in that village poem of twenty-five years later, *The Parish Register,* "Auburn and Eden can no more be found."

Unlike Wordsworth or the agricultural critic Cobbett, who also knew to what nearly bestial levels England's crumbling rural economy was reducing its country folk, Crabbe rejected all visions of apocalyptic regeneration in the English countryside. Antediluvian Auburn lay forever beyond because it was incontrovertibly before the experience of historical man. As a rebuke to imagemakers like Goldsmith, who encouraged a dream of what might once have been, or Cobbett or after him Carlyle, who were sure that happy valleys could be made to flourish again, Crabbe held up for examination the unhappy flatlands of East Suffolk and the darker penchants of man's nature. Crabbe's view of the peasant and his possibilities is closer to such anti-Romantic representations as Millet's in the painting which inspired Edwin Markham's famous poem (although Crabbe cannot share their post-Romantic suspicion that the peasant's enemy may simply be society):

> O'ercome by labour, and bow'd down by time,
> Feel you the barren flattery of a rhyme?
> Can poets soothe you, when you pine for bread,
> By winding myrtles round your ruin'd shed?

Intolerant of the discrepancy between daily life and pastoral art, Crabbe asks us to share his judgment that the muses have been able to sing so sweetly of

happy swains,

> Because the Muses never knew their pains.
> ....
> For no deep thought the trifling subjects ask:
> To sing of shepherds is an easy task.
> The happy youth assumes the common strain,
> A nymph his mistress, and himself a swain;
> With no sad scenes he clouds his tuneful prayer,
> But all, to look like her, is painted fair.

Crabbe's judgment is still somewhat naïve, as is generally the judgment of young men somewhat too early disillusioned. The pastoral dream, he believes, has survived in literature only because of deplorable ignorance and base dishonesty. So one who some years earlier has mourned, in *The Library*, the demise of heroic knights comes now before his public armed with truth and honesty and pledged to strip away the "tinsel trappings of poetic pride" and scourge the dragons of illusion which everywhere besiege the immature.

Whenever, therefore, Crabbe gives his "real-life" peasants pastoral labels, the reader's dismay is understandable but unnecessary. It is sometimes argued that Crabbe's occasional retention of diction common to the kind of verse he is attacking destroys the whole point of *The Village*. In truth, it reinforces the point. Like Spenser, whom he so much admired, Crabbe had and retained a taste for the strange flavor of contemporary language laced with outmoded diction. When he borrows "nymph" and "swain" from the poets' idylls that are his butt, he is often employing a kind of semantic irony. In this poem of ironies, the clash between what is and what poets pretend rings but more loudly when, for example, a pregnant woman and her seducer, pressed by a lascivious judge into a marriage that promises to be sordid, bring ironic overtones of pastoral to the courtroom:

> Lo! at his throne the silent nymph appears,
> Frail by her shape, but modest in her tears;
> And while she stands abash'd, with conscious eye,
> Some favorite female of her judge glides by,
> Who views with scornful glance the strumpet's fate,
> And thanks the stars that made her keeper great;

Near her the swain, about to bear for life
One certain evil, doubts 'twixt war and wife;
But, while the falt'ring damsel takes her oath,
Consents to wed, and so secures them both.

That Crabbe's most generous contemporary critic, Francis Jeffrey, questioned whether his "strokes of sarcasm" in this very passage had not perhaps reached beyond good taste[3] suggests that he, at any rate, had felt the lance of Crabbe's quaint diction used in defense of the truth.

During his later life, Crabbe, the sarcastic knight-errant, mellowed considerably; and humility and humor came to play major roles in his poetry; but he never ceased opposing reality (as he understood it) to illusion (as he defined it). An aspect of Crabbe's work that rings modern in our ears is his determination to expose all illusions, disperse all dreams, undermine most high hopes, and magnify facts. This preoccupation, often dictating the very structure of his poems, repellent to some of his readers and fascinating to others, receives in *The Village* its most passionate though not its most convincing expression. Again and again, in an astringent couplet or in a packed verse paragraph, Crabbe restates his conviction that what he learned during two decades in that neglected, sea-battered, unhappy village of Aldeburgh is the antidote which his readers must swallow if they wish to be cured of the dread disease of romanticism, one of whose symptoms is pastoralism:

cast by Fortune on a frowning coast,
Which neither groves nor happy valleys boast;
Where other cares than those the Muse relates,
And other shepherds dwell with other mates;
By such examples taught, I paint the Cot,
As Truth will paint it, and as Bards will not. . . .

Man's tendency to act as if whatever desirable thing his mind conceives might be or become real—this is Crabbe's enemy. We all recognize *some* degree of danger in such a tendency, and somewhere in *The Village* each of us feels at least a tremor of the shock of such a recognition.

Crabbe declares that he will truthfully "paint" the cot. He is using a verb more commonly applied to literature in his day than in ours, and it was through his celebrated "paintings" that his contemporaries were most likely to feel the shock of recognition. They enjoyed comparing him to Hogarth and to Flemish realists in oil. *The Village*'s antidotal illustrations include two darkly brilliant pictures of exteriors and interiors. One of these Wordsworth memorized while still in school, and so did Walter Scott—the sketch of the ill-built, decaying poorhouse into which were crowded the parish poor, young and old, who spend their days in squalor and misery, victims of, in Crabbe's words, "the cold charities of man to man." Wordsworth's unhappiness over what man has made of man must have given this grim phrase special significance for him, but the couplet he most admired was one near the end of the nine-line rollcall of inmates: "The lame, the blind, and, far the happiest they!/The moping idiot and the madman gay." At this point in Crabbe's life, as for the Wordsworth represented in the *Lyrical Ballads*, life must at times have seemed so intolerable for so many that insanity could be considered a blessing.

Equally good poetically is the painting of the village's neighboring landscape,

> where the heath, with withering brake grown o'er,
> Lends the light turf that warms the neighbouring poor;
> From thence a length of burning sand appears,
> Where the thin harvest waves its wither'd ears;
> Rank weeds, that every art and care defy,
> Reign o'er the land, and rob the blighted rye:
> There thistles stretch their prickly arms afar,
> And to the ragged infant threaten war;
> There poppies, nodding, mock the hope of toil;
> There the blue bugloss paints the sterile soil;
> Hardy and high, above the slender sheaf,
> The slimy mallow waves her silky leaf;
> O'er the young shoot the charlock throws a shade,
> And clasping tares cling round the sickly blade;
> With mingled tints the rocky coasts abound,
> And a sad splendour vainly shines around.

This, Crabbe's first real attempt at nature description, has seemed to some readers closer to science than to poetry. Crabbe, the amateur botanist, once collected the specimens it names; Crabbe, the recollecting and shaping artist, selected and arranged the rest of the words to exploit or to create certain musical and emotional values. But there is no doubt which Crabbe decided upon the modifiers *wither'd, slimy,* and *sickly;* conceived that progression of verbs in a darkening context, *lends, Reign, rob, threaten, mock, cling;* or chose to conclude with such words as *sad* and *vainly.* It was Crabbe, the untranquil recollector of emotion. No poet had ever before considered such a landscape quite fit to versify—probably no poet had ever before felt so strongly about such a landscape.

Although we suspect in Crabbe a genuine affection for this forbidding scene, he is purposefully presenting it as malevolent rather than merely infertile—as a landscape almost conscious of its own malevolence. It bears no more resemblance to the rich inland landscapes of pastoral poetry than do tradition's nymphs and swains to Crabbe's workworn counterparts, his farm laborers and fishermen and smugglers, the "bold, artful, surly, savage race" whom the poem presents as penniless, maltreated, diseased, rude, lascivious, hypocritical, and corrupt. Goldsmith, we remember, had seen his peasants as honest and golden hearted.

Read for its representation of characters from "low" life, for its landscape passages, or for its descriptions of interiors, *The Village* is arresting for handling unconventional subjects and for handling them unconventionally; and what arrests us, really, is the mark of Crabbe. His somber marsh, fen, heath, and coast; his poorhouse and its inmates; and his ill-educated, ill-mannered fishermen—all are as certainly reflections of his own state of mind as they are reflections of reality. The cumulative effect of *The Village* is emotional; the poem is an expressionistic painting rather than a photograph. It reflects not only Crabbe's discovery that art has betrayed life but also his bitter memories of an adolescence spent unhappily in an uncongenial place. The poem's most autobiographical passage tells how young Crabbe had trustingly but vainly sought in Aldeburgh "the simple life that Nature yields" but found instead only "Rapine and Wrong and Fear" and the "greedy sea." This sea, the unkempt village, and the insolent, insensitive natives of this "frowning" coast were all conspirators: all were in league against the struggling, sensitive doctor who was convinced that he deserved much better. Perhaps two years before he wrote this passage he had already deserted Aldeburgh: and, except for the four months spent as its curate early in 1782, he never took up residence there again. His exile from the borough he had come to hate actually endowed it with strangely large proportions in his memory. Like a forsaken beloved, Aldeburgh haunted him the rest of his life. Portions of *The Parish Register* (1807), all of *The Borough* (1810), some of *Tales* (1812), and much of *Posthumous Tales* (1834) are thinly disguised but more charitable studies of his deserted village.

Aldeburgh's surrounding landscape haunted him too, especially the sea, which colored his life even as it did his poetry and periodically drew him to its edge from whatever inland town he was living in. One summer's day in 1787, while engaged with his curacy at Stathern, he "was seized . . . with so intense a longing to see the sea, from which he had never before been so long absent, that he mounted his horse, rode along to the coast of Lincolnshire, sixty miles from his house, dipped in the waves that washed the beach of Aldborough, and returned to Stathern."[4] Cowper saw the hand of God wonderfully at work in the Midland landscapes, but the power of the sea over Crabbe lay somewhat otherwhere. He saw it as an enemy of man—as dangerous and definable as any man's own passions, with which, indeed, he frequently associated it. Inevitably, therefore, Crabbe saw something of himself in the sea. The "restless ocean," as he called it in a 1779 fragment, that "emblem of my mind," washes through his poetry to the very end, sometimes calm, sometimes wild, always glistening with implications. As insular a poet as the isle of Britain has ever produced, Crabbe was nevertheless early and forever marked by that seacoast and that shrinking village at whose mean and measurable streets licked the immeasurable, awesome sea—the "imperious" element which since Queen Elizabeth's day had diminished Aldeburgh by many streets. A year before his departure in 1780 one great tide had taken another eleven houses.

So much in love with Sarah and poetry and so out of love with his native place, Crabbe left home, Suffolk, and the sea for London with three pounds in his pocket. The swallows in *The Village* that poise rather unrealistically toward the right hour are not swallows in a simile but a gathering of Crabbes, for he has appropriated the simile to himself:

> As on their neighbouring beach yon swallows stand,
> And wait for favouring winds to leave the land,
> While still for flight the ready wing is spread:
> So waited I the favouring hour, and fled—
> Fled from these shores where guilt and famine reign,
> And cried, Ah! hapless they who still remain;
> Who still remain to hear the ocean roar. . . .

The Village is so urgently personal that its *saeva indignatio* is not fully trustworthy. Rude fisherman, devouring wave, street and marsh—these are villains in a dramatic projection of Crabbe's struggle, only recently concluded, for self-respect, even for survival. To the poem's subjective density we can attribute part of its individual flavor and most of what is original in it; but this vindictive subjectivity also plays havoc with the poem's structure and with the forms and modes it supposedly follows.

The historical-pastoral-satirical-tragical *Village* is an uncertain medley of various kinds of poem popular in its century: the disquisitional essay; the analytical or explanatory poem on a clearly defined concrete object or process; the character sketch; the landscape study; and, as reviewers in 1783 saw at once, the pastoral poem itself. Indebted to all these types, it can belong to none, not even to the topographical poem it most closely resembles.[5] Crabbe fails to maintain a clear sense of purpose throughout. *The Village* contains contradictions difficult to resolve, one of which actually derives from a "correction" by Johnson that Crabbe gratefully accepted. Halfway through the first book, for instance, Crabbe turns inland to exhibit a contrasting village not afflicted by "Nature's niggard hand," but it turns out to be virtually a duplicate of the village by the sea. In that seaside village, for another example, live men "sullen," "suspicious," "savage," and yet Crabbe has earlier in the poem attempted to evoke our pity and sympathy for these men. What can his reader do but suspend judgment altogether?

Similarly, Crabbe's scene of villagers reaping punishment for immorality comes as a non sequitur since what it follows is a declaration that village life is not always painful or disgusting. And, although he asks the idle rich whether they could endure such a difficult life as their poor hirelings live, he tells the poor not to envy the unhappy rich.

The confusion becomes ludicrous when, at the climax of his 553-line exposé of the pitiful state to which England's upper classes had allowed her rustics to decline, Crabbe begins to eulogize the wealthy nobility. He nominates as model for all mankind Lord Robert Manners, late son of the Marquis of Granby and younger brother of the Duke of Rutland, Crabbe's employer. Crabbe's mixed attitudes towards the villagers who had belittled him as a chemist's apprentice, as a doctor, and as a curate muddied his intended defense of the rustic against the pastoral's misrepresentations. We cannot excuse this defect in the poem, but we can tolerate it. Wholly intolerable, however, is the concluding flattery of Manners, so ill attached to the poem and so out of harmony with its supposed thesis—in fact, so dishonest. By thus servilely bowing to a literary convention and to his own hopes for preferment, Crabbe offends too seriously.

The *Eclectic Review* for January, 1809, forthrightly declared in a review of the 1807 reprinting of *The Village* that the poem ought to have ended exactly where the offensive panegyric begins. It really ought to have ended some lines earlier; for lines 101-6 are a bridge, however rickety, from Crabbe's real subject to a shameless betrayal of his hopes that the noble employer unearthed for him by Burke would become his patron too. Perhaps *The Village* once did end there; for, although it was begun in 1780 or 1781, it was not concluded until late in 1782, a few months after Crabbe had become the Duke's chaplain.

The poem may, in fact, have once ended a hundred lines earlier, with the opening couplet of Book II: "No longer truth, though shown in verse, disdain, But own the Village Life a life of pain." Most of the poem's contradictions lie between Books I and II or within Book II itself. At the end of Book I, Crabbe seems to have rounded off his poem rather well with two sketches of men briefly and uselessly attending a dying shepherd. One is a callous, greedy apothecary; the other a pleasure-loving, callous priest, an ironic contrast to Goldsmith's priest in *The Deserted Village*. These two type-figures are dim prototypes of the fuller-bodied, more individualized characters appearing in Crabbe's poetry almost a third of a century later. The faint pretense of a life history of the dying shepherd anticipates the narrative form Crabbe was working with in the last letters of *The Borough* (1810).

In *The Village* the two-dimensional figures and the unexceptional life story would have served their purposes well enough had the poem been 205 lines shorter. As the little group of mourners turns from the grave, troubled that the cynical priest has not stayed long enough to bless the dead man's bones, *The Village* reaches a credible, logical, indeed fitting stopping point. No shepherd in the bucolic tradition had ever been seriously affected by the passage of time; and, apart from pastoral elegy—a traditionally affirmative exercise—death had always lain beyond the horizon. Crabbe's brief account of the painful decline and forlorn death of the shepherd is thus one of his more striking rebukes. Futhermore, the two hasty officiators, one medical and one spiritual, give the poem's thesis a final underlining: the rustic is indeed a figure miserable and helpless in body and in soul.

If Crabbe decided, or was persuaded (perhaps by Burke), that another two hundred lines of more cheerful representations would increase the poem's verisimilitude, he failed to perform accordingly. The second book opens with a promise of relief but rapidly becomes as morbid as (and more confused than) the first. The two books do become, however, somewhat less incompatible if we avoid the mistake of reading Crabbe's passion for truth as humanitarian fervor. His sympathies in these years were sufficiently liberal to cause him to become—unlike his Whig patron, Burke—"one of the innumerable good men who . . . hailed the beginning of the French Revolution. . . ."[6] But his mind had already become too cautious to allow him to make wholehearted commitments. Mistrustful of all hotheadedness, Crabbe also knew that pure reason could reach the dangerous temperatures of a passion. Man is thus prey to excesses of both heart and head, and whatever pity Crabbe does feel for the poor of his *Village* is hardly distinguishable from the pity he feels for frail mankind.

Wordsworth, who long retained some of Rousseau's sentiments and many of Godwin's ideas, still regretted in his later years that Crabbe had not shared the reforming zeal of John Langhorne, an eighteenth-century poet who had left his mark upon both Wordsworth and Crabbe. In 1837 Wordsworth remarked of Langhorne's *Country Justice* (1774, -75, -77), that it had early brought "the Muse into the company of common life, to which it comes nearer than Goldsmith, and upon which it looks with a tender and enlightened humanity—and with a charitable, (and being so) philosophical and poetical construction that is too rarely found in the works of Crabbe."[7] Wordsworth's complaint here is that Crabbe's inclination is always to blame human nature for man's unhappiness. Langhorne and Wordsworth were inclined to blame society.

In *The Village* this assignment of blame is misleadingly managed. Not until Crabbe outgrew, in the nineteenth century, his obsession with poverty could he convincingly show that the proud and wealthy can be as guilty or as miserable as the poor and humble. This thesis is certainly not the poem's "dominant note," as Strang thought.[8] Rather, it lies submerged and breaks surface only occasionally, as when Crabbe remarks that in everyone, regardless of station or purse, we can

> the kindred vices trace
> Of a poor, blind, bewilder'd, erring race;
> Who, a short time in varied fortune past,
> Die, and are equal in the dust at last.

Despite the nearly neutralizing phrase "in varied fortune," three of the *Village*'s contradictions turn out, now, to be less serious. If vice may inhabit all men and if resistance to vice depends little upon social conditions, then those poor for whom Crabbe's verses waken compassion must as human beings receive also their share of reproof. The figure Envy in Crabbe's allegorical "The Birth of Flattery" (1807) twice lied when he "told the poor, what joys the great possess'd,/The great—

what calm content the cottage bless'd," but in *The Village* Crabbe is not so clear in declaring that the poor have less reason, after all, for envying their betters. Morally, he argues, their "betters" are their equals, and so a removal from barren seacoast to fertile inland means only a geographical change, not a moral one. The subject of Crabbe's scrutiny in *The Village* may seem a topographical one, but the poem contains evidence of Crabbe's inclination already to put his scrutiny to the service of his real subject: the moral and psychological topographies of mankind. This he does in later, better poetry; and, in doing so, he generally praises justice above mercy.

The most widespread misconception regarding *The Village* has been, despite corrective essays by various critics, that it is a kind of bombshell laying waste forever the lovely landscapes of the pastoral and leveling the pretty huts of its citizenry. Crabbe becomes thereby a kind of glowering knight whose chase had a real beast in view, and a blatant one. Crabbe himself might have been pleased had he wrought such a blow upon so ancient an enchantment, but human nature will not permit the pastoral dream ever to disappear altogether. Nearly fifty years after *The Village*, Crabbe recorded his awareness that the beast was not dead yet. In a long, uneven poem first published in 1960,[9] he administered his old rebuke upon the newer generation: "A Village then—let idle Poets cease/T'impose on Man— is not the Seat of Peace." And man goes on today hoping that he may yet leaven his oppressively metropolitan and industrial society with pastoral grace. Should even this hope wither, pastoral will not; for imagination is nearly as willing to dream backward as forwards.

The impulse towards pastoral has certainly not disappeared from our literature. It has only been modified. We have witnessed its continuing survival under more or less clear guise in such varied figures as Shelley, Arnold, Hardy, Yeats, Forster, D. H. Lawrence, Frost, Auden, Steinbeck, Tolkien. In fact, it did much more than survive Crabbe; within Crabbe's lifetime, it achieved through Wordsworth, the father of his century and a forefather of ours, a place of true distinction and influence such as it had not enjoyed since Milton. Each of us has been modified by those rustics whose humble names ought not to deceive us as to their pastoral identity—Matthew, Lucy, Michael, William.[10]

Crabbe's *Village* struck no deathblow; nor was it (another misconception) the decade's or even the century's solitary attempt to do so. It belongs to a long list of poems which, by exposing the preciosities of eighteenth-century pastoralism, helped prepare the way for a nineteenth-century pastoral revival labeled by its revivers as Realism. Oddly enough, probably "the most close and sustained analogue to Crabbe" in all eighteenth-century poetry is the charitable Langhorne's *Country Justice*.[11] Wordsworth was influenced by Langhorne's humanitarianism, for the poem is a plea for reform in the treatment of rustics and vagabonds, and Crabbe was influenced by the rhetoric of that exposure and by its narrative style. Langhorne must have encouraged both poets to introduce low characters into their poetry, for *Country Justice* contains gypsies, husbandless mothers, dying shepherds, and other outcasts. Dozens of other writers had already contributed in various ways to the new, though not self-conscious, school of antipastoral—Jonathan Swift, for instance, and John Gay and Samuel Johnson, to cite only some greater names.[12] Crabbe nevertheless approaches the subject with his own kind of passion and compassion; for, as Edmund Burke said of him at the time, he had the merit of thinking for himself. As a plea for truth above fancy, *The Village* is the most piquant single product of the school.

Among Lord Byron's various tributes to Crabbe, the most interesting appears in *English Bards and Scotch Reviewers* (1809):

> Truth sometimes will lend her noblest fires,
> And decorate the verse herself inspires:
> This fact in Virtue's name let Crabbe attest;
> Though nature's sternest painter, yet the best.

The epigrammatic fourth line was engraved upon Crabbe's tombstone in 1833 with "her" in place of "the"—an interesting mistake. *English Bards* came out a year before Crabbe published *The Borough*, where he first showed himself a nature poet of magnitude. What Byron did not say and could hardly have meant may, nevertheless, be true: Crabbe is one of English poetry's most powerful nature poets. But Byron, Neoclassical in

taste like Jeffrey, was happy to have in Crabbe a reputable contemporary poet who had gone to Pope for schooling and not
rebelled; and the word "nature" must have had for Byron
Neoclassical overtones, at the least, and meant something like
truth—faithfulness to human nature and to representative men in
representative settings. The conservative *Anti-Jacobin Review*
had said two years before, when reprinting a brilliant character
sketch from Crabbe's *Parish Register* in which no natural
setting appears: "He may most truly be called the poet of
nature who best delineates natural characters and natural
scenes; and certainly no one displays more skill, in this kind of
delineation, than Mr. Crabbe."[13]

It is an error, however, to assume that readers like Byron
admired Crabbe only because he was nostalgically quaint, or
praised him only because his popularity was a useful weapon
against the Lake School. Of all the aspects of Crabbe's later
poetry which *The Village* contains in traces, the most important
is the way description functions to create emotional meaning.
F. R. Leavis has said of Crabbe that "in the use of description
of nature and the environment generally, for emotional purposes
he surpasses any Romantic."[14] We must wait for Crabbe's later
work to find him using description for dramatic and psychological purposes, but it is used emotionally in *The Village,* where
its use is so personal as to be, perhaps, not always conscious.
Descriptions like that of the heath convey Crabbe's attitude
towards his subject as surely as does the confused expository
progess of the poem. The village of this "realistic" poem has with
some justification been called "probably the most individual
and concrete spot in all of eighteenth-century poetry," but
Crabbe held up to Aldeburgh more than the Neoclassist's mirror;
in Abrams' metaphoric terms, the village Crabbe seems so
concretely to "mirror" has been previously viewed by the glow
of the "lamp" of his own feelings, and it is a village "bathed in an
emotional light he himself has projected."[15]

The long-repeated claim that *The Village* is the destroyer of a
millennium-old convention may be appealing but it is ill-founded,
and the impression that the poem is Crabbe's masterwork may
be generally held but is utterly false. *The Village* must be read
for other reasons: because it is a famous contribution to the

literature of antipastoral; because, despite imperfect construction, it is an effective piece of expressionism; and because it is an articulate, if prejudiced, attack upon illusion. But, above all, it should be studied because this early poem by a major poet does anticipate a few of the qualities of Crabbe's future greatness.

II   *The Proper Point of View*

The superlative which Byron affixed to "painter" in characterizing Crabbe is too strong, for Crabbe is not our "sternest" painter in verse. But he is of the company of the stern, and he is so because he found that life required him to be so. The human situation, he early learned, is a precarious one. Men are as short-tempered as they are shortsighted, quick to mistake ill for good, folly for wisdom. Even careless gaiety is fatal—though not good humor and wit; for they are among the buttresses of sanity in a world where, Crabbe's tales go on reminding us, it is not easy to remain sane. Humor and wit are among the ways we adjust the thoughtless ebullience that is our birthmark to the burdensome perplexities, disenchantments, and disasters which the world discovers for us in our own lives and in the lives of others. In the 1780's, however, Crabbe was still too much the victim of a strange gloom to smile often.

The word "care," present in the opening lines of *The Village* and establishing at once the tonalities of that poem, still tolls occasionally in Crabbe's later work. It reverberates throughout the first section of *The Library* (1781), whose publication had been the first literary fruit of Burke's spontaneous and generous sponsorship. Burke had plucked Crabbe from the threat of imminent starvation or imprisonment and handed him in their place a profession, assurance of an income, and a publisher. Yet no more than *The Village* of two years later does *The Library* contain any of the exultation we would expect at such an extraordinary juncture in a young poet's life. Instead of elation, we find careworn cheerlessness—for, at best, the opening hundred iron-gray lines of *The Library* offer but the coldest of comforts. They argue, as an aesthetic applicable to some of Crabbe's work but not all, that literature refreshes us because it substitutes for our real worries and pains imaginary ones. Through a peculiar simile, Crabbe broaches the possibilities of relief for the "sad soul by care and grief oppressed. . . ." Periods wholly peaceful or serenely hopeful actually increase our unrest, he says, using a mirror-lamp image, even as windless seas distress sailors. The sailor knows that

> On the smooth mirror of the deep resides
> Reflected woe, and o'er unruffled tides
> The ghost of every former danger glides.
> Thus in the calms of life we only see
> A steadier image of our misery;
> But lively gales, and gently-clouded skies,
> Disperse the sad reflections as they rise;
> And busy thoughts, and little cares, prevail
> To ease the mind, when rest and reason fail.

So the remedy for our "stubborn sickness of the heart" (that "quiet desperation" which Thoreau saw as the tenor of most men's lives) is a perusal of "congenial cares" that are not our own. As therapeutic as the care-dispersing gales and clouds, all books that "lead us willing from ourselves, to see/Others more wretched, more undone than we" can "steal our grief away, and leave their own behind;/A lighter grief!"

Crabbe might have produced something remarkable had he organized the rest of *The Library* according to this mixture of Aristotelian "purgation" and the idea, later so well articulated by Coleridge, that we commit ourselves to fiction by temporarily and willingly suspending our disbelief. The aesthetic wherewith Crabbe grimly launches the subjects of books can apply, however, only to certain kinds of fiction; *The Library* by original plan must survey many categories of writing. Crabbe has soon to shift ground, developing the less interesting argument that reading teaches while it distracts, offers "mental physic" for "the diseas'd in mind" and salve for the "sickly soul." And soon we find ourselves perambulating the library aisles, "mansions of the dead," and listening to our narrator-guide pithily characterize the contents of the volumes we pass—botany, philosophy, medicine, law, history, drama—"mild opiates" all.

Just before we reach the cantankerous critics, whom Crabbe

for several reasons leaves until last, we come upon the shelves of romance or "fiction," a category which receives more attention than any other and prepares us both for the reappearance of the key word "care" and for the conclusion, as melancholy a meditation as that which opened the poem. The first and last quarters of *The Library,* in fact, are meaningfully related; the center floats between, attached to them and unified of itself only by the simpleminded plan of a tour of the stacks.

The imperfect *Village* offers throughout something of interest; the less imperfect *Library* does not. Crabbe's comments on the classes of learning can be incisive, as when he treats of religious controversy, or penetrating, as when he calmly explains without attacking "the true—not the sentimentally interpreted—doctrine of Rousseau's discourses";[16] and they are never downright dull. But the poem suffers from too mechanical a plan and from a sort of academic chill. Neater than *The Village,* better wrought, but less readable, this earlier poem is among the colder of Crabbe's productions. The chill that lies upon it is that of scepticism.

Five months after the publication of *The Library* Crabbe was a deacon; thirteen months after, an ordained priest. Yet the poem shows a spiritual malaise that may have approached despair. Traces of an intellectual and sometimes spiritual exhaustion are present in other poems of the period—poems composed between 1778 and 1780.[17] Crabbe had been nourished as a child on fairy tales, ghost stories, and prose romances; had later been beguiled, like so many other poets, by *The Faerie Queene;* and had become an imitator of the effete poetry being published in back pages of monthly journals. In short, he had once been, as he later admitted in the 1780 poem "To Mira," one of those "Dreamers of Dreams" who has no choice but someday to be awakened by "pale Disappointment." His earliest poems, peopled with Chloes and Damons and devoted to the "related" subjects of love and fame, are of the kind *The Village* ridicules.

Crabbe's love for Sarah undoubtedly helped insulate the young poet-dreamer against the onslaught of life in Suffolk—and we remember that *The Village* related pastoral nonsense to love's blindness. Crabbe concocted the nickname *Mira* from the second syllables of *Elmy* and *Sarah;* but *Mira* had also long been one of those perfumed names by whose means poets pastoralized their beloveds. In *"The Lover's Journey"* (*Tales*, X), a courting lover modeled expressly after young courting Crabbe rechristens his beloved *Laura*, a name from another but equally literary convention:

> Fancy and love that name assign'd to her,
> Call'd Susan in the parish-register;
> And he no more was John—his Laura gave
> The name *Orlando* to her faithful slave.

But how long could young Crabbe willingly suspend his disbelief and go on weaving out of his own imagination what he confessed in "The Choice" (1780) to be but "slender webs of wealth, and peace, and love,"—how long use as his map for life a "glowing chart of fairy-land?"

We cannot know whether Crabbe's fairyland faded slowly or rapidly; nor how much influence to attribute to the hostile sordidness of his environment, how much to the domestic turmoil his son guardedly refers to in the biography, how much to the natural readjustments that come with maturity, or to Crabbe's studies in botany, medicine, and philosophy, or to the frustration of his overlong engagement to Sarah. Each of these experiences furnished him with important subjects and themes for his later poetry, and certainly by his twenty-fourth birthday in December of 1778 he was sufficiently acquainted with desolation to write a pathetic birthday poem commemorating annual "woe" and "dread" instead of joy, a poem that looks forward only to a resumption of the "unconscious night" out of which he was once unhappily born.

Crabbe came to see, however, that the root cause of his depression did not lie in biographical particulars peculiar to his life. *The Library* shows him discovering that he has suffered—rather more severely than most—a fundamental human experience, one which may contribute as much to the making of a poet as does being born. "We do not begin to live," Yeats wrote, "until we conceive life as tragedy." Crabbe was experiencing the birthpangs of such a conception. He had discovered that growth implies disintegration; that gain can also be loss; that, even as feeling can betray mind, mind can contaminate feeling. Eventually this tragic sense of life was to bear much fruit, but at the time it seemed merely paralyzing. He was suffering, with no relief yet in sight, "the general doom" (*Borough*, IX), the "one fate at different times assign'd" all men (*Parish Register*, I). The pretty pastels of dreamlife that disappeared from his poetry forever were replaced by the grays and browns and blacks of a factual world where "they who most enjoy shall much endure" (*Parish Register*, II). Noting the "cool, neutral tone" with which Crabbe's tales of many years later generally begin, Lilian Haddakin added that, whatever his subject, the " 'temperature' may not rise far above the tepid throughout . . . ."[18] This characteristic tepidity has its cause in these formative years. The desperately jaunty metrics of "To Mira" conspire with the poem's conclusion to pretend that all can once again be cozy and gay, but Crabbe admits in the same poem "That Fortune has soil'd the gay Dress of each Dream;/ That Time has O'erthrown every fairy-built Scheme;/That thinking has slacken'd the Force of his Nerves," that, in short, the warmth of long-nourished illusions has vanished. He must henceforth live as he can in the colder temperatures of "reality."

Stubbornly honest, the disenchanted Crabbe would not deny what appeared to be fact. Much of the eighteenth-century literature he must have known was turning out to confirm what experience had taught. When he called himself, in an "Epistle to Prince William Henry" (April, 1780), a man "taught in hard affliction's school to bear/Life's ills, where every lesson costs a tear;/Who sees from thence the proper point of view," he had uppermost in mind his own career; but he was also remembering the dicta of his century's darker sages, savage Swift, for example, or melancholic Johnson. In "Drifting," one of the numerous poetic fragments dictated by his "gloomy Muse" of 1780, Crabbe says he has become

> Like some poor bark on the rough ocean tost,
> My rudder broken, and my compass lost,
> My sails the coarsest, and too thin to last,
> Pelted by rains, and bare to many a blast,
> My anchor, Hope, scarce fix'd enough to stay
> Where the strong current Grief sweeps all away . . . .

Some admirers of Crabbe's poetry think it unfortunate that he became a minister. Perhaps they are right, but it is erroneous to assume that Crabbe was wholly unfit for the profession. His "Prayers and Meditations" of 1780, printed in his son's *Life*, precede by a year his reminder to Burke of his "great inclination to the church." That adjective "great" is slightly suspect, for he knew and we know how useful to his stomach, purse, and poetry-making a minister's post could be. But in an earlier, unpublished essay of 1779,[19] Crabbe aimed to prove, step by step, the existence of God. That he felt the necessity to do so is significant; so is the fact that he made the attempt. Crabbe's religious preoccupations in this period may bespeak the depths to which the gnawing worm of disillusionment had reached; his readiness to enter the Church intimates that not everything had been gnawed away.

In one sense, Crabbe never fully recovered from what Strang a bit naïvely celebrated as the "healthy" scepticism of these years. Crabbe's lifelong war against enthusiasm, imagination, and the ideal remained truly an obsession. In another sense, however, he recovered brilliantly; and, as Strang more accurately concludes, "it was just that scepticism and that disillusion which make him what he is above all—a sincere poet."[20] Still, that word "sincere" needs some qualification; "true" would need less.

The first masterly chords the poet Crabbe struck are in the romance passages of *The Library*. Here his malaise found its fullest expression. To this poem's narrator, who is really Crabbe, there seems little left in the world to admire or even to trust. His dream world destroyed, honest Crabbe must ally himself with the destroyer, truth. In something like a state of shock, Crabbe seems now to see humanity as less attractive than the "torpid beetle, and the shrinking worm;/And insects," less vital than Carl Linnaeus' sexual parodies of man, those amorous flowers which Crabbe treats in lines that remind one of Erasmus Darwin.[21] Today, Crabbe realizes, man is at best frivolous; in earlier centuries he was no more than pedantic; and Rousseau's original "natural" man is as savage and rude as civilized man is deluded or corrupt. Even the wisest have been as often swayed by fashion as by truth: "man's best efforts taste of man, and show/The poor and troubled source from whence they flow . . . ." The natural sciences bewilder as they instruct. Law is shot through with error and evil. History, like philosophy, uncovers but the baseness of man's "progress." Theologians are dull if mild at heart; spiteful, if high-spirited. Crabbe's least unkind words are for the natural sciences. His bitterest are for the medical tomes, practical and theoretical. Over these poisonous deceivers, a "frigid tribe" of "treacherous leaders," the "first seducers of my easy heart," Crabbe had grubbed for years. He cannot forgive them for setting such "false fires" alight in him.

In *The Library* Crabbe seems, in fact, frost-locked, as if truth had been the face of Medusa. Nothing breaks the frost except "the ancient worthies of Romance." His apostrophe to them is a monument to the now disgraced power of imagination that grew in the garden from which reason's cold sword has driven him. Disgraced but not unwept, for Crabbe permits romance some melodious tears, composing as the only emotional portion of *The Library* an elegy for the qualities of youth forever lost. As he approaches the volumes of Romance, their "noble mien" and "awful grandeur" prepare us for the first twenty playful but atmospheric lines in which Crabbe allows to crowd round him once more "Ghosts, fairies, demons," knights and pages, giants, and all that the "potent wand" of "wild Enchantment" can evoke[22]—lines which Scott still had by heart twenty years after he read them. "Ah!" Crabbe exclaims, "Ah! happy he who thus in magic themes,/O'er worlds bewitch'd, in early rapture dreams. . . ." In his later work the words *enchantment, bewitch,* and *rapture* belong—like *passion, fiction, enthusiasm, imagination, fancy, wandering, gay*—to a group nearly always used pejoratively. In *The Library* they are still in the process of gathering their later connotations; they still trail, therefore, when they come, clouds of glory, the glory of the lost country of Romance:

> lost, for ever lost, to me these joys,
> Which Reason scatters, and which Time destroys;
> Too dearly bought, maturer Judgment calls
> My busied mind from tales and madrigals;
> My doughty Giants all are slain or fled,
> And all my Knights, blue, green, and yellow, dead;

No more the midnight Fairy tribe I view
All in the merry moonshine tipling dew;
Ev'n the last lingering fiction of the brain,
The church-yard Ghost, is now at rest again;
And all these wayward wanderings of my youth,
Fly Reason's power, and shun the light of Truth.

In 1783 Crabbe told Burke that, as an unhappy apothecary's clerk, he had at eighteen "read Romances and learned to bleed."[23] And forty years later Crabbe was to be famous as a maker of fiction that appealed to Scott, to Byron, and to the same public that found Scott's novels and Byron's narratives exciting. Crabbe even versified a few ghost stories for the 1819 *Tales of the Hall*. But now, unaware that life is not so dark as it may seem at twenty-five, and unpracticed in spiritual resilience, Crabbe was driven in extremity to question whether illusions—the child's, the lover's, the poet's, and perhaps the madman's, compacted as they are—were not preferable to truth. "Too dearly bought," the startling modifer of "Judgment" (the text being followed is that of 1781), anticipates the question raised in the next verse paragraph, as well as its regretfully negative answer. By now, the shelved romances have acquired such associations as to represent a great body of abstractions which Crabbe sees as related: feeling, imagination, childhood, innocence, happiness, even health. They may all have to be relinquished. The paragraph is ennobled by the courage with which it faces the fact that the tragedy of coming-of-age is its very necessity:

With Fiction then does real joy reside,
And is our Reason the delusive guide?
Is it then right to dream the Syrens sing?
Or mount enraptur'd on the Dragon's wing?
No, 'tis the infant mind, to care unknown,
That makes th' imagin'd paradise its own;
Soon as reflections in the bosom rise,
Light slumbers vanish from the clouded eyes;
The tear and smile, that once together rose,
Are then divorc'd; the head and heart are foes;
Enchantment bows to Wisdom's serious plan,
And pain and prudence make and mar the man.

We should now not only be looking back some fifteen years
to the boy's expulsion from paradise on the day of the excursion
up the Alde, but looking ahead some thirty-five years to Crabbe's
recording of this experience in "Infancy." It was a memory ever
demanding new expression in verse.

Childhood, like love and poetry, is no real paradise, only
an apparent one. On the other hand, disciplining judgment
comes too costly; reflection clouds our vision; and, whether it
is pain or prudence that mars the man, all is not well with
wisdom's serious plan. The same suspicion comes to the reader
of such poems by Langhorne as the second book of *The Enlarge-
ment of the Mind* (1765). Langhorne and Crabbe, familiar with
the work of the associationist philosopher David Hartley, prepare
one for Wordsworth's great and, despite all the efforts of the
explicators, still ambivalent Immortality Ode. Crabbe understood as well as Wordsworth that the sundering of head and
heart—that "dissociation" placed by T. S. Eliot in the midst of
the seventeenth century—is not so certainly an historical event
as a universal phenomenon, or at least the fruitful curse of all
born into Western European civilization. Crabbe repeatedly
warns against the havoc wrought by uncontrolled feeling and
yet frequently writes to the effect that only feeling can "give
the tongue the language of the heart" (*Tales of the Hall*, V).

The Library in 1781 accepts reluctantly as inevitable and *The
Village* in 1783 wholeheartedly what *The Candidate* of 1780
refuses to accept. In addressing himself as a poetic aspirant to
the renowned critics of the *Monthly Review*, Crabbe in this
poem glorified "the tints that beam on Fancy's bow" and "the
fires on Genius' wings." He identified himself as a member
of the "wild and visionary race" of poets; and, while naming
"honest truth" his inspirer, he indicated that this "truth" is
really the "transports" of love and hope. Especially is love his
"soul's resistless lord," who

> Shall many a gentle, generous strain afford,
> To all the soil of sooty passions blind,
> Pure as embracing angels, and as kind;
> Our Mira's name in future times shall shine
> And—though the harshest—Shepherds envy mine.

Under Cupid's power, he offers an almost Keatsian prospectus, promising that he will "Of laughing girls in smiling couplets tell,/And paint the dark-brow'd grove, where wood-nymphs dwell . . . ." The villains of his later work—enthusiasm, rapture, the "syren-song" of the enchanting pastoral muse—are this poem's idols. Self-consciousness, reflection, judgment are the villains. Iconoclasts whom he cannot bear to face, they threaten to question all he holds sacred—nature, art, love.

> Ah! tell men not these empty joys to fly;
> If they deceive, I would deluded die;
> To the fond themes my heart so early wed,
> So soon in life to blooming visions led,
> So prone to run the vague uncertain course—
> 'Tis more than death to think of a divorce.

By now—probably 1778-79—Crabbe already fears that reason and passion are turning antipathetical; in *The Library*, where "divorc'd" appears in a thematically comparable position, he is to mourn their having already turned so. He is there to admit that innocence is irretrievably lost. In *The Candidate* he dwells on the time when fancy was never weakened even by doubts; when "No guilty dreams stalk'd that heaven-favour'd round,/ Heaven-guarded too,"; when "No sceptic art veil'd Pride in Truth's disguise . . . ." Crabbe rises in this poem to eloquent pathos whenever he expresses, prophetically, his fear of desiccation, of being reduced to telling over and over, like worn beads, what he elsewhere calls—in "Time" (1780)—the "paralysing tale" of misery and care.

The *Critical Review* for September, 1780, treated *The Candidate* most acidly, misrepresenting its content and caviling over minor points of style and grammar. The *Monthly Review*, also for September, criticized more kindly, perhaps because the poem was addressed to it. But the review ended with the serious complaint that the poem lacked a subject. It has a subject—one which nineteenth- and twentieth-century poets have made us more sympathetic to. Its subject is Crabbe himself. The poem is a brief, primitive *essai*, Crabbe's first but not his last, in tracing the growth of his own mind. Crabbe was too young to know that his mind had a long way still to grow, and he was too inexpert to realize that his subject needed concrete material instead of fanciful disgressions of a conventional sort.

The earlier *Inebriety* (1775) is in some ways a more impressive performance. It dates from his years as apprentice to a surgeon in Woodbridge, Suffolk. Reflecting nowhere his current courtship of Sarah, who lived in neighboring Parham, it derives instead from evenings spent with young friends in a Woodbridge inn.[24] It is so rowdy, satiric, and irreverent a poem that Crabbe's son suppressed its third part. If portions of the more personal, meditative *Candidate* and *Library* belong to the associational strain that Locke and Hartley had fostered in eighteenth-century poetry, *Inebriety* belongs to another, much older strain: the impulse towards flamboyant realism native to the English. This impulse was gathering a peculiar kind of force and tone in the eighteenth century, but it had long been flavoring English literature—as far back as Chaucer and Medieval liturgical drama, it had erupted spontaneously in low-life characters, scenes, and behavior. Crabbe's tippling vicar is not handled with Chaucer's delicate humor and is clearly an eighteenth-century figure, even type; but, when we meet him, we realize that he would be at home among the Pilgrims:

> The Vicar at the table's front presides,
> Whose presence a monastic life derides;
> The reverend Wig, in sideway order plac'd,
> The reverend Band, by rubric stains disgrac'd,
> The leering Eye, in wayward circles roll'd,
> Mark him the Pastor of a jovial Fold,
> Whose various texts excite a loud applause,
> Favouring the Bottle, and the good old Cause.

Close cousin to the raucous comic scenes of the cycle plays is Crabbe's scene describing the drunkard's return from the tavern, a description darkened by Crabbe's memories of Aldeburgh and his familiarity with corrosive satirists of his own century—Hogarth, say. In mock heroics that sustain the allusions to bombastic provincial puppet shows, Crabbe tells how the drunkard awakens the rage of "his sleeping Rib" by thundering madly on their hovel's walls. This "buxom Quean" descends and "civil war" breaks out; the "Hero" wields an oaken club in his defense and the awakened baby shrills throughout. Calm returns only when the man and his wife have battered each other into exhaustion.

Inebriety seems to have received no critical attention at all, but it was a promising beginning. Its versification is uneven, its taste questionable, its subject inelegant—but all this is inseparable from the poem's great virtue, its vigor. Pope, whom a fifth of the 718-line poem indirectly compliments by directly burlesquing, had provided Crabbe with a verse form which he retained to the end of his career, transforming it to fit his later needs. The era provided the vehicle, the essay on a single subject; and this Crabbe retained for more than half his career, until he dispensed with it wholly in the *Tales* (1812). The real weakness of *Inebriety* lies in its being a pastiche. Among the authentic lower-class laborers, hypocritical clergymen, and tavern dolls there float, as if they could not find their graves, pale alien ghosts of poets Crabbe has been reading—Milton, Gay, Gray, Young, and pastoral pipers. The poem's realism cannot assimilate such a figure as the Miltonic rustic full of nut-brown "Ale and content," one "happy Colin," who, while the wind whistles outside, sits drinking by the embers and

> tells the Tale, from sire to son retold,
> Of spirits vanishing near hidden gold;
> Of moon-clad Imps, that tremble by the dew,
> Who skim the air, or glide o'er waters blue.
> The throng invisible, that doubtless float
> By mould'ring Tombs, and o'er the stagnant moat;
> Fays dimly glancing on the russet plain,
> And all the dreadful nothing of the Green.

This pastoral storyteller recalls to us the Crabbe who in *The Library* and in *The Candidate* could recall himself as he was before the reign of care began. *Inebriety* exposes, with a physician's scorn rather than with a minister's dismay, the folly of drink; but Crabbe actually blesses one of the drinkers because he resembles himself. Colin's "muddy ale," we are told, is like the poet's muse, and so "Peace be to such, the happiest and the best."

If Yeats was right and life begins only with the tragic vision,

Crabbe stood on the brink of life about 1779. He had painfully acquired the proper point of view, for such is the evidence of *Inebriety, The Candidate,* and *The Library.* But something kept him long in check, poised in a hardening stasis. Pastiche though it be, the youthful *Inebriety* boded better things for Crabbe as poet than the poem whose publication in 1785 marked the beginning of twenty years of silence. Technically admirable, the poem entitled *The Newspaper* is Crabbe's dullest production. It is as if the frigidity he had feared had at last set in.

This sarcastic attack upon periodicals is well conducted, is clear and sharp; but it could hardly arouse interest in anyone besides students of the history of journalism. *The Newspaper* could have been composed by any of the century's skilled practitioners of the couplet. Its peculiar subject allows Crabbe's accuracy of observation and knowledge of human nature very little play. His poem's main characters are newspapers, and they are handled only as types—the "base" insect hordes of Heralds, Posts, Gazettes, Ledgers, and Chronicles that titillate, scandalize, poison, or bore the multitudes. Crabbe does manage some grotesque humor, as when introducing a Sunday newspaper that pretends sanctimoniousness, the "sainted Monitor"

> Whose pious face some sacred texts adorn:
> As artful sinners cloak the secret sin,
> To veil with seeming grace the guile within;
> So Moral Essays in his front appear,
> But all is carnal business in the rear,

but such humor fails to sustain the burden of the whole. Crabbe's kind of epigram—thoughtful rather than brilliant, accurate rather than polished, wedded to context rather than detachable—was admirably suited to the complex texture of his later tales but could not salvage *The Newspaper*:

> Those, who ne'er deign'd their Bible to peruse,
> Would think it hard to be denied their news . . . .
> ....
> Grave politicians look for facts alone,
> And gravely add conjectures of their own . . . .

Provoked by a clash between liberals and conservatives in 1784, this poem is a political protest and an elegy; but the protest is so veiled, the elegy so muted, that neither is recognizable. Charles Fox's resounding defeat in election had brought even Burke, a close friend, into disrepute; and Crabbe felt impelled to offer his patron public testimony of his own sympathy. Just what, though, could the moderately liberal chaplain in the Tory household of the Duke of Rutland have to say about the defeat of a radical Whig? Not very much. *The Newspaper* avoids all topical issues, confining itself to satirizing such general phenomena as the violence of party strife and the influence of cheap journalism upon public opinion. Avoiding any hint of party sympathies, it denies itself the vigor of partisanship.

The only place where Crabbe's self and voice come through to us distinctly is the conclusion, in which the current of personal opinion, elsewhere short circuited by his obligations in conflicting directions, flows for the moment freely. He unexpectedly returns in it to his decade-long preoccupation with fancy, poetry, and living poets; and now we find him alarmingly cynical. Mere scribblers, foolish and deceived, he calls the would-be poets among whom only four years before he was one. When their poems appear, as a number of his had done, in the poets' corner of a magazine, that "fatal nursery for an infant Muse," they are simply entombing themselves alive. Their aesthetic inclination is a "wretched bias of the brain," their daydreams a "snare," their raptures an "evil spirit" in disguise, their occupation a spreading "infection." And should they happen to become successful, they must viciously rejoice to discover that their "dark pages please th' enlighten'd age." He who chooses poetry will be as miserable as he who is trapped into marrying a coquette. All young poetasters ought to turn from the Muse to Mammon, Crabbe savagely advises:

> Go! to your desks and counters all return;
> Your sonnets scatter, your acrostics burn;
> Trade, and be rich . . . .

Better yet, they should inherit money. Money, not poetry, is the root of all fame.

These painful passages are proof, if further were needed, that life had wounded Crabbe—harsh Crabbe, as he is so often called. But sensitive he must indeed have been to have become so harsh so young. Crabbe retained his sensitivity to the end, but the writer of *The Newspaper* seems an emotionally drained man. Perhaps, rather, he was a poetically drained one, who needed a new subject or a new way of seeing his old subject or a new form. He had acquired enough of all three by his next volume, the *Poems* of 1807, to let us realize that, when Crabbe as publishing poet began his long hibernation, he was entering a period of regeneration. He began late to discover, like Wordsworth, Yeats, and Wallace Stevens, that although the poet cannot alter the tragic condition of life he can defend himself against it.

CHAPTER 3

Expansions

I *The Reverend George Crabbe, LL.B.*

BEGUN in 1802, *The Parish Register* was completed in 1806; *The Borough,* completed in 1809, was begun in 1804. During the two overlapping years, Crabbe also composed at least two "lyrical ballads": "Sir Eustace Grey," published in the 1807 *Poems* with the *Register,* and "Hester," published in 1960. Among these four works are some obvious similarities and some more curious ones. Both sorts present us with a new Crabbe. Few men remain untouched either by the greater ideological movements of their generation or by the passage of time itself. Crabbe's essential character, molded before the last decade of the eighteenth century, was elastic enough to become modified between then and his reappearance in print in 1807. His life during these years—his threefold role as minister, husband, and father—wrought alterations in his character and hence in his poetry. So did the shifting currents of the age.

Most of "Hester" is flat material, but the poem has interest as one of Crabbe's attempts to imitate the new generation of Romantics—and even more interest for showing his inability to judge the quality of such infrequent and self-conscious attempts. The reformed prostitute Hester, who narrates before a chorus of unaccountably interested castle maidens a long account of her fall from virtue, is related to the unhappy heroines of the School of Sensibility and to the female outcasts immortalized in the *Lyrical Ballads* of 1798 but popular in the poetry columns of journals throughout the 1790's and even in the 1780's. The year Wordsworth and Coleridge published their volume, Crabbe wrote the first draft of another stanzaic ballad; and this one's central figure is also a vagrant woman with an horrific past. Revised, it appeared in the *Poems* as "The Hall of Justice," a

kind of companion piece to the better known "Sir Eustace."
All three ballads are the work of one who dares declare his
vulnerability to a new though not yet wholly respectable literary
fashion—to its interest in the social exile, in incest, in murder, in
prostitution, in emotionalism, and in association as a structural
device. Scott, himself a balladmaker, called "Sir Eustace" and
"Justice" works of "prodigious talent"; William Gifford of the
Quarterly Review called "Sir Eustace" a poem "second to few
modern productions."[1] Later on, Romantics-fed readers like
George Gilfillan, leader of the Spasmodics, praised the extraordinary force and horror of both "Sir Eustace" and—
Crabbe's best venture of this sort—"The World of Dreams," not
published until 1834.

Like the later works " 'Twas in a Country" (published in
1904) and the fragment "Where Am I Now?" (published in
1960), "Sir Eustace" is rich in images of dream and delirium,
but its narrator, an adulterer and murderer and the inmate of
a madhouse, expresses himself with psychologically inappropriate lucidity. His fantastic dreams have been considered the
result of Crabbe's opium-taking and must reflect something of
Sarah's advanced insanity, but the poem has a studied air in
no way reminiscent of the unconscious associations at work in,
for instance, Coleridge's "Kubla Khan."[2] Crabbe must always
define madness as a late stage of a common but dangerous
phenomenon—uncontrolled enthusiasm, whether religious, philosophical, sexual, or literary. The bias of the poem's vocabulary
presses us to pass orthodox moral judgment upon Sir Eustace
and prevents us from "enjoying" his fantasies.

Crabbe's genuinely Romantic tendencies do not appear in
his rather stiff and uncommitted imitations of the new school.
When he decided to seem Romantic, he could not permit himself to be so; when he was writing poetry he knew seemed
Augustan, his native romanticism, joining hands at times with
Romanticism, suffered less repression. Some of the effects that
Crabbe could not wholeheartedly work for in his undisguised
imitations we find instead in *The Parish Register* and, especially,
in *The Borough*—in, for instance, the couplets which handle
the sorrowful story in the *Register* of Phoebe Dawson and in
the description of the Lady's hall, or, in *The Borough*, the

gruesome career of Peter Grimes and the numerous descriptions of the sea.

Actually, Crabbe in 1807 was in no position to champion, had he wished to, the attitudes and sensibilities of the new, suspiciously revolutionary poets. A significant example of repression betrayed by revision appears in the revised version of *The Library* which Crabbe prepared for its 1807 reappearance. He altered it so heavily that, in comparison, the few dozen changes in the reprinted *Village* and *Newspaper* are negligible. The 1781 testament of scepticism has been reworked into a testament of belief.[3] Crabbe's ordination in 1781, Burke's financial solution for the would-be poet who would not be a doctor, had made *The Library* of just a few months before somewhat indecorously secular; but Crabbe could hardly now omit it from the 1807 volume, as he did his racy *Inebriety* and ill-received *Candidate*, both published anonymously and long ago forgotten. *The Library* was also an anonymous publication, but it had been identified at once as the work of Burke's promising protegé and had since maintained some slight reputation.

Like Crabbe's failure to commit himself to Romanticism, the revisions which convert *The Library* into the work of a poet who trusts religion above science, trusts received faith above experimentation, are due in part to Crabbe's temperamental inclinations and in part to his position as a cleric of twenty-five years' standing. But they also reflect the rapidly changed atmosphere in England between 1785 and 1800. Eighteenth-century liberal theorizing on matters religious, political, and moral—encouraged by the growth of the sciences—had begun in the last third of the century to take concrete forms alarming to vested interests—commercial, clerical, governmental, and social. Especially alarming was the French Revolution, which as it commenced had seemed a triumphant justification of these liberal principles nursed, like vipers, by the supposedly conservative Age of Reason. The reaction was violent. As the century approached its close, the conservatives' concerted attack in books, journals, and newspapers managed to swing public opinion so thoroughly against the scientists and philosophers of the new radicalism that men like the "atheist" Tom Paine and that sinister high priest of reason William Godwin and the evolutionist Erasmus Darwin[4] found themselves plunged within a decade from fame to infamy.

Cautious and reasonable as Crabbe was, he could not help being influenced by these angry, frightened voices of reaction. Since their clamor was in the name of state, church, and morality, "The Rev. George Crabbe, LL.B." of the *Poems'* title page could not remain indifferent. A case in point is a botanical passage in the 1781 *Library* that may have influenced Darwin. His long poem *The Loves of the Plants* was highly acclaimed when it appeared in 1789, but by 1800 it had been condemned as a work by a subversive heretic. Crabbe's botanical passage reappears in 1807 so altered as not to be an anticipation of Darwin's poem but a criticism of it. To be sceptical of anything long established was in those days practically to announce oneself as a potential enemy of crown and Church, social and moral order, England and Englishmen. It would be most unfitting for verses by the rector of Muston to resemble those by one of the land's archenemies.

In the Preface to the 1807 *Poems* Crabbe allowed more space for praise of Burke, then dead ten years but still famous for having been respectably conservative in his response to the French Revolution, than for praise of Fox, yet alive, a friend, an advisor in poetical matters, and one whose political opinions, including opposition to England's engaging France in war, Crabbe had more recently shared. He also felt it necessary to explain why his volume contains no religious or patriotic exhortations. His reason is suspiciously simple: I am not adept with such themes. His more interesting Preface to *The Borough,* three years later, is in places more laboriously cautious. Almost any of its many paragraphs justifying the treatment of subjects or characters he fears to be offensive illustrates well his elaborate prefatory precautions:

If I have in one Letter praised the good-humour of a man confessedly too inattentive to business, and, in another, if I have written somewhat sarcastically of "The brick-floored parlour which the butcher lets:" be credit given to me, that in the one case I had no intention to apologize for idleness, nor any design in the other to treat with contempt the resources of the poor. The good-humour is considered as

the consolation of disappointment, and the room is so mentioned because the lodger is vain. Most of my readers will perceive this; but
I shall be sorry if by any I am supposed to make pleas for the vices
of men, or treat their wants and infirmities with derision or with
disdain.

To read this mannered prose, characteristic of Crabbe's prefaces
(though not of his letters), is to become somewhat reconciled to
the loss of his three novels.

Crabbe had even to be careful in handling the earthier side
of man, which clearly attracted him. The popular reactionary
views of law and class were accompanied by a moral squeamish-
ness to which the School of Sensibility, once handmaid to
radicalism, now catered. Freethinkers were seen to relate political
experimentation and moral latitude; the lower class's Methodism
seemed a cousin to anarchy; and, through the influence of
naughty France, sex and revolution were virtually considered
siblings.

In adjusting himself to all this, the minister-poet sometimes
overplayed his hand. The decline of *The Borough's* simpleminded Abel Keene begins when he becomes a sceptic; it concludes in suicide because he has been influenced by a Calvinist
preacher. One of the proofs given by Blaney's hopeless depravity,
in the same work, is his fondness for Voltaire. The sequence of
ten disasters that, in another book of *The Borough*, fall upon
Ellen Orford because she let her lover seduce her includes her
husband's hanging himself while under the influence of Cal-
vinism and one of her son's being hanged on the gallows because his reading of Godwin had turned him into a criminal.
When the narrator of *The Parish Register* says that a local
atheist calls "the wants of rogues the rights of man," the point
of Crabbe's reference to Paine's famous work is clear. Crabbe
is also playing for the conservatives' applause when he declares
in his own voice, in *The Borough*, that "Men are not equal, and
'tis meet and right/That robes and titles our respect excite."

But such overanxious bows to orthodox opinion, with some
of which Crabbe surely concurred, do not hide another Crabbe,
one to whom the simple judgments of unexamined orthodoxy
are distasteful. To these "robes and titles," symbols of the order

necessary to the wellbeing even of a democracy, we need only juxtapose those robed lawyers and judges of Crabbe's poetry whose greed or hypocrisy ruin good and simple men, or the seductions practiced by the invulnerable nobility upon innocent girls from the lower classes. Ellen's son may be damned for reading Godwin, but Crabbe shows elsewhere a Godwinian dismay over a penal code that condemns honest men to long prison terms because they have fallen into debt. The good-natured Abel fell quick victim to temptation, but Crabbe is amiably scornful of his borough vicar whose virtue rests in its never having been tested. Although the *Monthly Review* felt that Crabbe too frequently denounced irreverence towards the clergy, the *Eclectic Review,* shocked by the "levity" in his handling of religious subjects throughout *The Borough,* admitted genius in the Reverend Crabbe but would not vouch for his characters, concluding, "We must own the performance appears to us almost certain to do some harm, and almost incapable of doing any good. . . ."[5]

Ellen's terrible punishment gives her elementary sexual offense the color of something unspeakable, but Crabbe alludes to far more depraved matters in his sketches of Clelia, whose long and thoroughly spotty career includes the seduction of widowers for whom she keeps a boardinghouse; of Frederick, a drunken actor, thief, and pimp; and of Blaney, in the piling up of whose monstrosities Crabbe hints at subjects not to be treated openly in literature until Zola and Büchner. In his handling of these three figures, Crabbe as much understates the evils as he overstates them in handling Ellen; and in the fifth book of *Tales of the Hall* he does not disguise his view that for a woman to be seduced by her lover is less sinful than for her to accept a proposal of marriage from a licentious, unloving courter.

Another kind of contrast to the melodramatic moralizing of "Ellen Orford" (a subject to be resumed later in the chapter) is Crabbe's use of sex for comedy. The comedy is never quite discreet. He satirizes, for example, the timidity of such passionless men as his borough vicar, who is constitutionally unable to perform a full-blooded courtship and therefore is happier in the company of elderly women. Such men are "Nature's soft

substitutes," "lilies male" who might better be employed guard-
ing the "treasures" of seraglios, Crabbe says—"An easy duty,
and its own reward." Sexually disreputable persons are as often
made amusing as odious, like the "aunt" of the borough's Bear
Inn and her interminable succession of "nieces." The most odious
ones are men who marry in old age. Crabbe was rebuked by
both the *Edinburgh Review* and the *Eclectic Review* for the
suggestive metaphors that describe in the *Register* the impotency
of elderly bridegrooms. Crabbe's anxiety not to offend led him
promptly to revise the passage for the next year's edition.

The sexual comedy can be downright bawdy. Crabbe uses
for his tale of Juliet Hart and her Romeo, James, an allusion
to a tale by Boccaccio as a comment upon Shakespeare's pair,
that most romantic of all loving couples:

> The nymph was gentle, of her favours free,
> Ev'n at a word—no Rosalind was she;
> Nor, like that other Juliet, tried his truth
> With—"Be thy purpose marriage, gentle youth?"
> But him received, and heard his tender tale,
> When sang the lark, and when the nightingale;
> So in few months the generous lass was seen
> I' the way that all the Capulets had been.

What follows (for the story is but half over) is Realism's comment even upon Boccaccio. James avoids Juliet and her parents
for ten or more months; when he does return, his motives are
fear of law and pity for Juliet. The parents are no more perfect
than the erring couple; but, since all four have natures of
sufficient warmth, the tale has a happy ending. Bickering leads
to reconciliation, and they all look forward with satisfaction to
a double ceremony as Juliet joyfully addresses her illegitimate
infant: ". . . thou shalt grace (bedeck'd in garments gay)/The
christening-dinner on the wedding day." The *Eclectic Review*
censured Crabbe for the whole tale.

Despite numerous pressures to conform to the narrowed
judgments of his age, the Reverend Crabbe remains independent;
for "this gnarled and sea-salted man," as Virginia Woolf has
said, "was no smug clergyman underneath."[6] The reason he was
none such is given us bare when at the conclusion of *The*

Borough he announces that he is to all men "a fellow, not a foe—/A fellow-sinner, who must rather dread/The bolt, than hurl it at another's head." Patrick Cruttwell interprets the deep insecurities of the surrealistic "World of Dreams" as "a phantasmagoria of the whole of Crabbe's essential life," and Geoffrey Grigson sees not only the opium-drowned Sir Eustace but also the ostracized Jachin and the sadistic Peter Grimes of *The Borough* as autobiographical guilt figures.[7] If Cruttwell and the more extreme Grigson are right, Crabbe's heroic couplets seethe with tensions of a sort we like to consider rather modern.

Crabbe's inability to stifle his own often heterodox insights is more important than his attempts to seem conventional; and it has left a greater mark upon his poetry. To appreciate his insight and his brand of sincerity, today's reader must remember that the revolutionary theorizing of men like Charles Darwin, Marx, and Freud had not yet called seriously into question, for better or for worse, centuries-old assumptions. Their systematic interpretations of man as a physical, a political, and a psychological creature lie between us and Crabbe. And yet his skill in tracing human motives to their covert sources makes him seem post-Freudian; and, since he has been claimed in France at least[8] as an important literary influence upon nineteenth-century social reforms, he may be placed among those agitating forces that lead from Godwin's age to the era of Marx—a placement that would surely startle Crabbe himself. And, finally, his geological vision of life was such that he could compose for *Tales of the Hall* (Book XIII) a passage whose content suggests the impossible, that he had been reading Charles Darwin, but does prove that he had taken Charles' grandfather, Erasmus, seriously after all:

> He rode to Farley Grange and Finley Mere,
> That house so ancient, and that lake so clear:
> He rode to Ripley through that river gay,
> Where in the shallow stream the loaches play,
> And stony fragments stay the winding stream,
> And gilded pebbles at the bottom gleam,
> Giving their yellow surface to the sun,
> And making proud the waters as they run.
> It is a lovely place, and at the side

Rises a mountain-rock in rugged pride;
And in that rock are shapes of shells, and forms
Of creatures in old worlds, of nameless worms,
Whose generations lived and died ere man,
A worm of other class, to crawl began.

The river's gaiety and the pride of water and rock should
not be dismissed as pathetic fallacies. In context, they convey
a sense of nonhuman organic significances equal, if not even
superior, to those of man, who is seen in such a perspective
as only one more worm among numberless kinds. Yet that last
line's "worm" returns us to Crabbe as moralist. The difficult
road we travel with him in his collected works is that of one
who can examine man with the dispassion of botanist, doctor,
and geologist, with the abiding scepticism that fastens upon
an early-disillusioned romantic, and with the empathy of the
artist—and yet never lose his moral vision of man as a responsible
creature.

II   Good and Evil Mix'd

The two decades of parish work which were to supply Crabbe
with much of the information crammed into his *Borough* also
suggested the idea for the longest new poem in the 1807 *Poems.*
The Parish Register may have seemed a quite fitting product
from the already aging hanger-on of the old school, for what
could be a more likely device for the Reverend Crabbe's new
work than that of having a priest turn the leaves of his parish
register; glance through the names of all who during the
year had been born, had married, or had died; reminisce upon
the memorable ones; and then gather the reminiscences into
three parts: "Baptisms," "Marriages," and "Burials," all versified
in heroic couplets. This survey device allies the *Register* superficially to Crabbe's eighteenth-century essays; and, when we
learn from the opening lines that we are to "explore/The simple
annals of the parish poor," we begin to wonder if any time
has passed since Crabbe published his other poem on village
life.

"No Muse I ask," he announces, "before my view to bring/The
humble actions of the swains I sing," and very soon we come

upon another familiar announcement: the cloudless, rustic land "of love, of liberty and ease," (Auburn or Eden) is a place known only to poets and not to *this* one. Crabbe had been remembered for his attack upon deceiving fancy, for the repellant realism of his "paintings," and for the pathos he could wring from poverty. The *Register*, it was clear, offered its readers something again of all three. Was it, then, to be but the second telling of a tale twice told?

Crabbe identified the *Register* in his 1807 Preface as "an endeavour once more to describe Village-manners" as they actually are, and he accordingly put *The Village* first in the volume and the *Register* directly after. Then come the reprinted *Library* and *Newspaper*, then the rest of the new poems: "The Birth of Flattery," "Reflections," "Sir Eustace Grey," "The Hall of Justice," and "Woman!" So the reviewers are to be excused for extracting for quotation from the *Register* a long description of the foul row of buildings where dwell the town's poor. This passage had most reminded them of that still remembered *succès d'estime*—his *Village*. This is how the legend perpetuated by Hazlitt began, that Crabbe—joyless, humorless, heartless—relished only ugliness and misery.

The two poems are, however, more unlike than alike. The new Crabbe is, for one thing, a poet whose focus is no longer upon general subjects—newspapers, drunkenness, a village, a library; it is not now even upon a parish but upon the human figures in the foreground, upon character drawing and the rudiments of narrative. And not only has the priest of long standing failed to bludgeon the poet into pietism or even encouraged him to be abjectly intimidated by the time's peculiar climate, but the poet's temperament has, in fact, undergone an alteration; so that the work of the new Crabbe shows fruitful modification of that earlier, essentially "proper" but unalleviated, too binding point of view. Not that the *Register* is not afflicted with melancholia too, as its plan of moving from baptisms to burials suggests at once and as Crabbe admits, in a voice of quiet lamentation:

> When these my records I reflecting read,
> And find what ills these numerous births succeed;
> What powerful griefs these nuptial ties attend,

> With what regret these painful journeys end;
> When from the cradle to the grave I look,
> Mine I conceive a melancholy book.

Still, Crabbe has forgotten at the commencement of "Burials," where this passage lies, that the melancholy of two-thirds of his book has already been diminished by episodes of delicate sentiment, light satire, and comedy. As when one's eyes have grown accustomed to a loss of light and can rediscover things once known but mislaid, Crabbe had come to see that life includes much he had excluded from *The Village*. It is a matter of stress, after all, an oscillation between "With what regret these *painful* journeys end" and "With what *regret* these painful journeys end." All is not grimness, atrophy, or total loss—Crabbe had made himself say this in *The Village* but had failed to demonstrate it. That heavily subjective poem has, in consequence, a morose, dank grandeur which the *Register* does not; but what the *Register* may lack in grandeur, it much more than makes up for in credibility, craftsmanship, and scope. Like *The Borough*, it illustrates what Crabbe in a four-verse paragraph early declares: the world contains "good and evil mix'd"— but, he adds, "man has skill/And power to part them, when he feels the will!" Then, in a typical gambit, Crabbe at once checks whatever enthusiasm these words may have aroused lest we assume in man an equal proportion of weakness and strength: "Toil, care and patience bless th' abstemious few,/Fear, shame, and want the thoughtless herd persue." Like his honest lawyer (rare specimen in Crabbe!) in *The Borough*'s sixth letter, Crabbe has found so much baseness in man that now

> He knows how interest can asunder rend
> The bond of parent, master, guardian, friend. . . .
> ....
> Sound in himself, yet, when such flaws appear,
> He doubts of all, and learns that self to fear:
> For where so dark the moral view is grown,
> A timid conscience trembles for her own;
> The pitchy taint of general vice is such
> As daubs the fancy. . . .

Even so, the voice that speaks from *The Borough* and *The Parish Register* is not that which spoke from *The Village*. The colors of Crabbe's world will never be bathed in the sudden spring sunlights of Chaucer's world, but the temper of Crabbe's work has begun to move in Chaucer's direction (even in technique), which by the concluding letters of *The Borough* will show us a Crabbe soon to realize his destiny as a maker of verse narratives surpassed among English poets by Chaucer alone.[9]

The good humor which many of Crabbe's contemporaries found in the man himself is given sufficient outlet in his *Parish Register*. Jeffrey exaggerated only slightly when he praised the poem for its "many gleams of gaiety."[10] Sometimes this "gaiety" lies in situation. Gerard Ablett of "Baptisms" has been blessed with a prolific wife who produces a child for him every year. As a young bridegroom, he had followed his parson's recital of the service: be fruitful, multiply. But the multiplication got out of hand, and the blessing has worn thin. About his house now runs a troop of children whose antics and expense darken his days, for they "keep the sunshine of good humor out." Now this year his wife has produced twins, "a girl, a boy,/Th' o'erflowing cup of Gerard Ablett's joy." Crabbe presents all this in reversed chronology; only towards the end do we realize that what overflowed from that cup was a draught of superfluity less sweet than bitter.

More often Crabbe's humor lies in character portrayal, sometimes quiet, as when Donald resists laundry girl and dairymaid, sets his cap for the housekeeper, and wins both her and a butlership; and sometimes it is grotesque, as when tottering Nathan Kirk takes a young harlot as his bride. Crabbe can turn to comic use such things as the furnishings of Catherine Lloyd's house, her pets, the handwriting in his parish register, even language itself, the Latinical-botanical vocabulary which Peter Pratt, affected gardener, loves to mouth and insists on using as names for all his children—Lonicera, Belladonna, Hyacinthus. Most frequently, however, Crabbe's humor takes the form of quick thrusts, ironic turns, understatements, unexpected wry remarks passed before fully perceived—sometimes in units as brief as "forced a frank look" and "pomp obsequious." "Read me some amusing thing," Scott once told a friend, "—read me a bit of Crabbe." Even much of the "darkness" in Crabbe is "a satiric, that is a comic, darkness."[11] The wit that flickers upon every page of the *Register* and could never properly be extracted for sampling is proof that the new Crabbe is no longer plagued by an inordinate amount of bile.

The opening letter of *The Borough* ends with a promise of material varied enough to arouse now a sigh, now a smile; but, even before the earlier *Parish Register* begins, Crabbe informs us rather heavily of his now more sanguine temperament. The prose Introduction tells us that he has included consideration of the "State of the Peasantry as meliorated by Frugality and Industry." The poem's sixth line reminds us that the dead are lost not only to life's pains but to its pleasures; and our first picture of parish life is, in the words of the Argument, that of "The Cottage of an industrious Peasant; its Ornaments— Prints and Books—the Garden; its Satisfactions. . . ." Crabbe devotes lines 31-165 to this material, but they are the least interesting in the poem. He has not after all quite escaped, in this section, the shadow of his own *Village;* it vitiates the *Register's* first pages. This opening effort at melioration is too self-conscious, remains poetically stillborn. More lively by far is the contrasting passage on the weak-willed, shameless, indolent poor, the passage so much admired by reviewers who had remembered *The Village.*

It was contrary to Crabbe's insight and technique to handle good unmixed with evil, beauty untainted by flaw, happiness untouched by misgivings. He constructs complexes of words, phrases, clauses, even passages which so qualify each other, generally ironically, that nothing is "pure."[12] Examples of this technique, congenial to the modern reader, abound in the tales of 1812 and 1819; but such fine work Crabbe managed nearly as well on the smaller looms of the *Register.* The account in "Baptisms" of why and how a workhouse boy rose to wealth and knighthood and then effected a deathbed reprisal is too long to reproduce in full. Its opening quarter, however, illustrates what fine stuff indeed this "Pope in worsted stockings," as two contemporary parodists dubbed Crabbe, could produce:

To name an infant meet our village-sires,

> Assembled all, as such event requires;
> Frequent and full, the rural sages sate,
> And speakers many urged the long debate.
> Some harden'd knaves, who roved the country round,
> Had left a babe within the parish-bound.—
> First, of the fact they question'd—"Was it true?"
> The child was brought—"What then remain'd to do?"
> "Was't dead or living?" This was fairly proved:
> 'Twas pinch'd, it roar'd, and every doubt removed.
> Then by what name th' unwelcome guest to call
> Was long a question, and it posed them all;
> For he who lent it to a babe unknown,
> Censorious men might take it for his own:
> They look'd about, they gravely spoke to all,
> And not one Richard answer'd to the call.
> Next they inquired the day, when, passing by,
> Th' unlucky peasant heard the stranger's cry:
> This known, how food and raiment they might give,
> Was next debated—for the rogue would live;
> At last, with all their words and work content,
> Back to their homes the prudent vestry went,
> And Richard Monday to the workhouse sent.

As the rest of the account confirms, the village sires (parish vestrymen obligated to attend to foundlings) have really done the child no kind turn by handing it over to be reared amidst the cruelties of workhouse life and, eventually, an enforced apprenticeship. We side with Richard. Although he develops into a hypocritical, hardhearted moneymaker, we are pleased when he violates parish law by fleeing apprenticeship, succeeds elsewhere in business, and becomes Sir Richard. We are gratified when his will, lavishly kind to groups whose gratitude might catapult him heavenward after all, leaves but an insulting pittance to the parish which reared him.

In this total situation evil is mixed with good—perhaps also in the moral response Crabbe permits us to make. The mixing begins even as the sires gather to perform an act of communal philanthropy. Does, for example, the rhyme word "requires" receive only accidentally its emphatic position? This fleeting question Crabbe answers in many ways. One of the more obvious is the phrase "unwelcome guest." The sires are behaving at first appearance as if the baby were an inanimate and objectionable thing on exhibit or some stray creature, unclassified but harmless enough to be pinched and tweaked. Over what, then, do these vestrymen, officious and "prudent," debate at length? Their chief concern is naming the boy. For this delicate problem Crabbe allows them six lines (and amusingly withholds for seven more one of the names chosen); for the apparently less important matter of keeping Richard clothed and fed he allows them, appropriately, two.

In the clause "for the rogue would live," the word *would* (instead of the more likely *will* or the more sarcastic *might*) is an example of how busily at work unobtrusive elements of Crabbe's language can be. New meanings for the clause insinuate themselves as we identify each overtone of *would*: "Despite the child's previous exposure and public handling, it seems a healthy creature," "Were it to starve to death, someone might impute to us vestrymen a regrettable laxity," and "If only it might die during or soon after our period of debate, the problems it has raised would be satisfactorily settled." All this is no more accidental than the position of "requires" or than the metrical surprise in the last line of the passage. The third line of a triplet has by convention six feet instead of five—Crabbe often used this means of achieving variety amidst strings of heroic couplets. But this particular third line lacks even the distinct fifth foot upon which the self-righteous vestrymen have just trooped home, for now the metrics imitate the vestrymen in brusquely dismissing Richard Monday to his fate.

The perceptions revealed by Crabbe's techniques of glancing ironies are based upon a rockbed of disillusionment. He is always more successful, therefore, when dealing with unmitigated evil or ugliness than with unmitigated goodness or beauty. Crabbe confessed as much in the sixth letter of *The Borough*: "a Muse like mine, to satire prone,/Would fail in themes where there is praise alone." Once in a while he did attempt praise alone, and the result in the *Register* is either flabbiness, as in his opening description of the good peasant's cottage, or sentimentality, as in his sketch of the golden-hearted, pure-souled Isaac Ashford, placed for relief and reassurance after the sketches of three coldhearted, selfish women. This "wise good man" Isaac, "contented to be poor," impressed Crabbe's audience to a degree that baffles us. It helps to realize, however, that Isaac is one of a crowd of literary figures relished by the reading public for a full century—from before Goldsmith up at least to Dickens—for being vigilantly self-effacing, benevolent, pious, and lachrymose.

Let us not, advised the *Gentleman's Review* for 1807, waste much time with those three "eccentric Females" but move to a "deserving theme," the smiles and tears of Isaac Ashford.[13] To us more interesting than Isaac, more deserving thematically and handled in poetry more arresting, are the three females: the Widow Goe, the unnamed Lady of the Hall, and Catherine Lloyd. These three sketches are also useful for illustrating three related aspects of the *Register*: the complexity of its structure, the variety of its material, and the deviations from the universal which its frequent generalizations about persons and life are able to contain.

Although Crabbe did not realize fully the possibilities of the *Register*'s simple plan, he made good use of it for variety. He could assume a voice long familiar to him, the parson's; but, because it is also a narrator's voice, he could fuse the first-person essay, with its subjective tones and moral emphases, and the third-person report of character and situation, with its description, dialogue, and simple action. In fact, most of the *Register* is "report." Of the remainder, most is meditative essay, so that only a very small portion of the whole is parsonical exhortation. Crabbe introduces and intersperses each third of his poem with abstract reflections on poverty, temptation, death; but he spends far more of his time storytelling, reporting how age is making Lodge a fool, how virtue has made Sir Edward Archer virtuous, or how love may yet make Lucy the miller's daughter mad.

Seven of the twenty-four parts of *The Borough* and nearly all of the twenty-one tales of 1812 are full-fledged short stories in verse. The *Register* has none; but at least three of its twenty-nine vignettes, as they may best be called, lie at the threshold of the short story. The chronologically straightforward account of Lucy in "Baptisms" begins at the time when her nautical suitor first heard of her, moves rapidly through the lively courtship, the parental refusal, the seduction, the pregnancy, the sailor's departure and death, and concludes with the forlorn girl's approach toward madness. The tale of Roger Cuff in "Burials" is structurally more sophisticated, and the tale of Phoebe Dawson in "Marriages" is the most affective of the three—it so moved Charles Fox when he read it in manuscript that he asked when he was dying to have it read aloud to him.

The rest of the vignettes may be divided into three overlapping types. Most common is the anecdote—either a highly compressed narrative like that of Lucy Collins' preference for fancy Daniel, which leads only to her unfortunate return to Stephen; or else a truncated narrative like the account of how the unschooled but trusted and efficient midwife Leah Cousins is replaced by the more modern doctor who is well trained but arrogant and possibly no more efficient. Our interest in these anecdotes lies equally in character and in novelty of situation.

A less frequent and less complex type is the character sketch in which action or situation takes second place—the examination, for instance, of the relationship between the happily married Robert and Susan or the study of that "valued Mother and a faithful Wife," Mrs. Frankford. Finally, there are vignettes whose purpose is only to illustrate some theme or to pose some problem. To this type belong the passage on the squire and his "ever-smiling bride" who have been forced by gossip into marriage and the description of the sullen "boy-bridegroom" and a girl in a maternity frock, so wretched that she but "faintly tried to smile"—these two have been forced into marriage by legal warrant.

Within any type, Crabbe approaches his material in various ways—through description of dress and face and gesture; through rapid summary of events or, in contrast, concentration upon one event; through comment upon personality traits; and through dialogue. The *Register* seems infinitely various next to *The Village*. A satisfying example of Crabbe's progress is the remarkable difference between the lone shepherd's formal soliloquy in that poem and the *Register*'s monologic *tour de force*, Old Dibble's address to his parson. Crabbe's "real" shepherd, imagined to be muttering to himself as he mends a hedge during a morning blizzard, speaks in accents just as unnatural, in their theatrical way, as those of pastoral poetry. He goes on for twenty fluent lines, about sixteen beyond the credible. The loquacious Dibble speaks 135 uninterrupted lines, and we are sorry when he stops. He surveys the life and character of each of the five parsons he has, as sexton, over the years served and buried; and, as he surveys their characters, he betrays his own—talkative, deferential, and no fool—"civil but sly," says the parson-narrator as Dibble archly smiles to think he may yet bury his sixth, who is, of course, our listening parson-narrator.

The Village gave no promise of what we also find in the *Register*: rudiments of verse dialogue of a kind peculiar to Crabbe's best tales. Crabbe is now beginning to manipulate rhythm, syntax, sound, and diction to reveal various speakers' character and role, as in the speeches of innocent, harassed Lucy, her breezy sailor fiancé, and her choleric father.[14] But Crabbe is also beginning characteristically to blur the usual clear distinctions between direct address, indirect address, and narrative, so that speech sometimes has the quality, even the grammar, of narrative (the sketch of Barnaby in "Baptisms"), and narrative sometimes the effect of speech (the sketches of Richard Monday in "Baptisms," Andrew Collett in "Burials").

In tone, as much as in anything else, the *Register* is impressively varied. Even more significant than Crabbe's alternations of passages distinctly satiric, pathetic, tragic, nostalgic, and comic are his exercises in varying a theme. For instance, the accounts of Phoebe Dawson and Lucy the miller's daughter are quite distinguishable even though similar in plot, theme, and final emphasis. Both girls are courted, seduced, and abandoned by lovers who sail away; both become husbandless mothers, go into exile, and are last seen on the edge of insanity. Phoebe's story, without monologue or dialogue, is almost exclusively devoted to developing her rather simple character, and its pathos is unrelieved by humor of incident, character, or diction. Lucy's contains three dozen spoken lines, develops two other characters, and is frequently amusing. Crabbe's numerically most extensive exercise in variation by particularization is that quintet of sextons in Dibble's monologue, but the longest and subtlest is the trio of "eccentric Females," dismissed in the lump by the *Gentleman's Review*. They do have much in common. All three are well-to-do and now aging women either unmarried or long widowed. A natural selfishness, abhorring the vacuum of their later years, has become their dominant, corrosive trait. Each, now in "the sad summer of her slow decay," faces death.

What all three do not have in common two may have. The Lady of the Hall and Catherine Lloyd share an unwillingness to aid the poor, and their unwillingness is criticized in direct speech by townsfolk. Catherine Lloyd and the Widow Goe are so attached to their possessions that each approaches death with special reluctance, the needles of their iron souls caught by the magnet of this world even as they try to face the other way:

> "Bless me! I die, and not a warning giv'n,—
> With *much* to do on Earth, and ALL for Heav'n!—
> No reparation for my soul's affairs,
> No leave petition'd for the barn's repairs;
> Accounts perplex'd, my interest yet unpaid,
> My mind unsettled, and my will unmade;—
> A lawyer, haste, and in your way, a priest;
> And let me die in one good work at least."
> She spake, and, trembling, dropp'd upon her knees,
> Heaven in her eye, and in her hand her keys;
> And still the more she found her life decay,
> With greater force she grasp'd those signs of sway;
> Then fell and died!—In haste her sons drew near,
> And dropp'd, in haste, the tributary tear;
> Then from th' adhering clasp the keys unbound,
> And consolation for their sorrows found.

The Widow Goe's sons cannot be deeply moved by the loss of a mother whose tyrannies alive bequeath them such monies dead; the parish poor cannot be moved by the death of the rich Lady of the Hall who remained indifferent to them when she was alive.

As clear as the reluctance with which these two women face death are their differing reactions to the problem of worldly allegiances. The Widow falls and dies an absolute hypocrite, attempting to disguise from others, even from herself, that only what she cannot take with her into death has any reality for her. Catherine Lloyd frankly confesses her failure and, however futilely, asks for guidance as the end approaches. Crabbe also discriminates between Catherine's indifference to the poor and that of the Lady. The poor have long hated and cursed the Lady for denying them the succor her position and wealth ought to have made obligatory. In contrast, Catherine wins the scorn of neither reader nor the poor when she dies. She is awarded, instead, a degree of pity. Her self-interest has in later years manifested itself in nothing more serious than coveting what one has—the silks, jewels, chests, and ivories once given her (gossip knows why) by a male "cousin." Introduced as "wise, austere, and nice," she has become ostentatiously careful to show "her virtue by her scorn of vice." The heart she allowed to become involved in an *affair de coeur* years ago had once been, we soon infer, warm and less virtuous. Chilled by succeeding decades of maidenhood, it now beats quickly only in the presence of select lady friends who appreciate the museum her small, neat house has become—they appreciate especially her imported crockery, whose "pictured wealth of China and Japan,/ Like its cold mistress, shunn'd the eye of man." In this sketch Crabbe does, indeed, exhibit "force and energy of intellect" by means of an almost feminine "finesse" as he paints "upon two inches of ivory with Miss Austen's brush of camel's hair."[15]

Catherine, though hardly a lively sort, seems sprightly next to the Lady of the Hall. We are told less about the Lady's life or character, for this vignette is an exercise in atmosphere. A "winter-death" lies over the Lady's fireless, cheerless country mansion, a tomb empty save for worms, bats, and the echoes of beggars rattling the bolted door. To this hall she comes only rarely for token interviews with her unhappy tenants, but after the interviews she sits in some inner room, as in a vault, insulated from the tenants by a mediating servant who prevents any complaint from reaching her directly. "The feeling servant spared the feeble dame"—context defines what this servant "feels," and it is as unsavory as the Lady's self-indulgence masking as feebleness.

The whole vignette is lugubrious. Over it Crabbe has cast the pall of a repellent, emasculated Gothicism that evokes no thrill or wonder, only disgust. The description of the Lady's

elaborate funeral sustains the tenor of the earlier passages on
her dreary house. There she had sat dead to sympathy while
her officiator conveyed her feigned concern; now she lies cof-
fined while

> Dark but not awful, dismal but yet mean,
> With anxious bustle moves the cumbrous scene;
> Presents no objects tender or profound,
> But spreads its cold unmeaning gloom around.

The last we see of the heroine of this study in cobweb, crêpe,
and coffin is a long-entombed, now "dissolving" corpse, "a mass"
which "fancy loathes and worms themselves disdain." The point
of this exercise after the manner of the Graveyard School, is
perfectly clear—too bad that Crabbe couldn't leave well enough
alone but had to make a village father, at the end, baldly, pub-
licly, and pompously draw the moral.

The Widow Goe has a vitality missing in both Catherine
and the Lady, and so therefore has her sketch. The Recluse
of the Hall, a horrid mass in death, was hardly more than
a stone effigy in life. And Catherine is a case of arrested development. She fell in love with the acquisitions of her lover after
the lover had disappeared, and the treasures became a kind
of revered tombstone, her tight-lipped savoring of them a testi-
monial. Shades of the tomb lie over her house too. But an
energetic self-interest assailed Mrs. Goe as soon as she put on
her widow's weeds:

> She lost her husband when their loves were young,
> But kept her farm, her credit, and her tongue;
> Full thirty years she ruled, with matchless skill,
> With guiding judgment and resistless will . . . .
>
> No parish-business in the place could stir,
> Without direction or assent from her;
> In turn she took each office as it fell,
> Knew all their duties, and discharged them well;
> The lazy vagrants in her presence shook,
> And pregnant damsels fear'd her stern rebuke;
> She look'd on want with judgment clear and cool,
> And felt with reason and bestow'd by rule . . . .

Since a quarter of "Burials" is taken up by these three women whom the *Gentleman's Magazine* significantly stigmatized as "eccentric," the *Eclectic Review*'s preference for "Burials" is worth attention, and so is its reviewer's first two and a half pages. The *Register* plunged him, apparently, into a critical reverie of surprising sort. No two human beings, he writes, no two faces or oak leaves or blades of grass have "ever so nearly resembled each other, that they could not easily have been discriminated on comparison." Less alike, he argues, are any two human minds; everything under the sun is different from every other thing, and every mind perceives everything differently. These observations could, we feel, be preparing the way for an eighteenth-century admonition that the artist's duty is therefore so to arrange or rearrange life's particularities as to illuminate what is typical or "normal" or ideal. The *Register* excited other thoughts, however:

He, therefore, who would delight the world as a Poet, must first learn to look at Nature with his own eyes, and he will soon discover wonders and beauties in her aspect, of which he was never aware, while he squinted at her through the "spectacles of books," and beheld nothing but tawdry, indistinct, and mutilated distortions of her simple and exquisite charms. But he must not only see, he must feel, and above all, he must think, for himself, with unperverted susceptibility of heart, and unshaken independence of soul . . . .

Poets and their readers, the critic continues, are mortal. "Immutability belongs to God alone." The true poet's work offers us, among familiar ideas and objects, a sufficiently impressive quantity of unfamiliar ones. Crabbe may lack "fancy, fervour, grace, and feelings"; but, because he has "Strength, spirit, truth, and discrimination," his readers can "see the distinct image of Nature herself reflected from the mirror of his individual mind . . . ."[16]

Crabbe is here being praised for placing nature's impulse to particularize above man's impulse to classify, and he is being admired for using a "mirror" which is pretty close to being the Romantics' lamp. Johnson, admirer of *The Village*, had declared (in his "Preface to Shakespeare," for instance) that art is meaningful only if it generalizes, because only generalizations carry equal import for all readers. Reynolds, at whose house Crabbe first met Johnson, had demonstrated in his third "Discourse" that serious deviations from established norms were mere deformities inappropriate to art. Crabbe retained to the end a strong interest in those types and patterns of objects, behavior, and experience which, being universals, his young manhood's mentors had considered the subjects of art. But this did not prevent his developing an interest in the deviation, in eccentricity, and in downright deformity, an interest that lead him to territories beyond the Neoclassicist's prescribed pale. Justifying his "Sir Eustace Grey," he first observes in the 1807 Preface that only Shakespeare is considered great enough to deal with madness; then he pleads, "Yet be it granted to one who dares not to pass the boundary fixed for common minds, at least to step near to the tremendous verge, and form some idea of the terrors that are stalking in the interdicted space." The elevation of Crabbe's prose here bespeaks his interest in this most horrific of deviations, an interest confirmed in a few years by the several studies of madness in *The Borough*.

To many readers in 1807 the author of *The Register* must have seemed to be moving towards "forbidden" things. Most solicitous to present Crabbe as an uncorrupted Augustan, Jeffrey nevertheless felt compelled to express uneasiness over some of his tendencies, noting that the vignettes "are finished with much more minuteness and detail . . . than the more general pictures in 'The Village'; and, on this account, may appear occasionally deficient in comprehension, or in dignity."[17] Jeffrey spent the rest of the paragraph trying to assure us—and, we are sure, himself—that this tendency deplorable in other poets is acceptable in Crabbe. So eager was Crabbe at times to uncover distinctions that what begins as classification may end as obliteration of classification. An amusing example appears in the eleventh letter of *The Borough,* where he spends 160 lines classifying two of the town's four kinds of inn. The first kind contains as many subdivisions, three, as it does inns; and, when he moves on to the third kind, he begins, "Next are a lower kind, yet not so low/But they, among them, their distinctions know."

In defense of *The Register,* Jeffrey pleaded its purpose of surveying village life entire, but his inability to appreciate its "minuteness and detail" prevented him from appreciating its numerous methods of organization. The first half of "Burials" is an aesthetic unit, its parts meaningfully related. On either side of the three eccentric women lie characters in partial contrast to them and in absolute contrast to each other: Andrew Collett, the "blind, fat landlord of the Old Crown Inn," and Isaac Ashford. Collett, defender of immorality and defier of law, is an extreme of selfishness, worldliness, and callousness. Ashford is an extreme of selflessness, spirituality, and sentiment. The forty lines on the death of babies that separate the Widow Goe from the Lady of the Hall only seem irrelevant, for they are related in theme to both women and to their half of "Burials." These forty lines prolong the attention paid at the conclusion of Goe's sketch to man as a creature of dying generations, and they treat of charity, which all three women lack. They also argue the spiritual advantages of living long enough to experience adulthood's afflictions, advantages the three women have had but have failed to make use of.

The Register owes something of its architectonics to Crabbe's growing interest in the ingredients of narrative, including character drawing, and something to his widened experience. The two are related. Both imply a degree of objectivity. Although the vignettes of *The Register* are embedded in a moral context that almost labels them *exempla*, Crabbe shows some reluctance to pass direct judgments upon figures in his human pageant. Every vignette has somewhere a deducible moral, and to some of them Crabbe affixes a passage that points the moral out (although generally less clumsily than with the Lady of the Hall). But like the "sub-Christian atmosphere" which is the result of his not pressing the Christian values he assumes,[18] his earlier sonorous moralizing is now dissolving into a pervading flavor. His attitude is likely to be expressed indirectly, by innuendo or overtone or structural and contextual controls. Even these oblique devices may sometimes seem obvious. The unnamed savage infidel, whose death brings five unbaptized children before the parson-narrator, had long lived by "Deadman's Dykeway" in "Lonely-wood," from which ominously named place he had sent his offspring out to practice free love and had himself roved abroad to blaspheme, thieve, and gamble. We surely do not need to be told that

> him our drunkards as their champion raised,
> Their bishop call'd, and as their hero praised;
> Though most, when sober, and the rest, when sick,
> Had little question whence his bishopric.

Yet even here Crabbe does not try to prove that theology's Satan is in control of this man who, finally, abroad to no good purpose on a wild night, fell into a swollen river, drowned, and "slept, if truth were his, th' eternal sleep." With that "if" the parish priest demurs. We are left with only what Forster has identified as the flavor of disapproval.

This sketch of an infidel concludes "Baptism"; it therefore directly precedes "Marriages." "Marriages," *The Register's* middle third, is immediately followed by the sketch of Collett, another infidel. This blasphemous frame emphasizes that marriage is a holy event, and we feel the force of the contrast. But we also remember that of the nine marriages sandwiched between the infidels, six are unsatisfactory or disastrous. We cannot say that the "contrast" has finally proved much—except that this intermixture of good and evil is what gives life that complexity which life's organizer, the artist, delights to take as his subject.

III *Man as He Is*

Like *The Parish Register, The Borough* (1810) offers a gallery of persons bound together by social, economical, and geographical ties. But now Crabbe also handles the binding ties, some in considerable detail. Instead of the engaged narrators of *The Register* and of *The Village*, he uses an unengaged citizen who examines varied aspects of his community by describing them in a set of twenty-four "letters" to an interested friend somewhere in the country. The shift from the parson's list of parishioners to an entire borough—its setting, institutions, and inhabitants seen as individuals and as groups—is a shift towards sociology. We are told how personal relations run berserk during borough elections, how local doctors and lawyers handle their work, how the poor are housed and treated, how the citizens pass their leisure hours, what diversity of clubs, inns, and religious sects the borough boasts.

Crabbe's sociological view of man in a community—stronger than Chaucer's or Dryden's—owes something, of course, to the vestigal Augustan habit of preferring averages to exceptions, types to individuals. It owes more to Crabbe's awareness that social forces help shape personality, just as personalities do social structures. Consider some of the reasons why Abel Keene changes from a "quiet simple man" to a suicide case. In his new role as office clerk, Keene tries, in late middle life, to become one of the boys. Turned "outer-directed" too late for his conscience's health, however, he begins to drown his qualms in excesses. His shocked sister points out how drastically his behavior denies the values of family life, and he flees her sermonizing. Later, his conscience is rearoused by the disgrace of having to apply for public charity, and it is finally so fatally sharpened by Calvinist doctrine that he hangs himself in a peddler's shed. Office, home, poor laws, and sect have made their contributions to this suicide.

The Borough's sociological pretensions were not wholly successful, as its reviewers intimated and as Crabbe himself may have begun to realize as he approached the later portions of the work. The best things in such earlier letters as "Trades," "Amusements," and "Clubs and Social Meetings" are the illustrative scenes and characters. In their composition the satirist and psychologist overrule the sociologist. *The Borough*'s best letters are those in which psychological and moral insights join to trace in detail the career of a single person, such as the lily-livered vicar; Denys Brand and each of his three favorites—the monstrous Blaney, the depraved Clelia, and the decadent Benbow; or the pitiful parish clerk, Jachin, apprehended for stealing the weekly collection money; or Peter Grimes, whose viciousness has contributed to the deaths of three successive apprentices.

Characters like Abel Keene are not the absolute victims of sociological forces, not the "puppets of an overpowering destiny; or the instruments of some . . . cunning Devil," as the *Monthly Review* complained they were.[19] Unhappy in his foolish pursuit of pleasures—for "pangs attend the birth of unbelief"—and "with

himself at war,/Far gone, yet frightened that he went so far,"
Abel has chosen to fall; and the pity of his decline is that he
has realized his freedom of choice from the first. Crabbe is
not a determinist, but he may be "at bottom a true Calvinist,"
as Paul Elmer More suggested, "showing that peculiar form of
fatalism which still finds it possible to magnify the free will, and
to avoid the limp surrender of determinism."[20]

Although *The Register* is *The Borough*'s parent and *The Village* its grandparent, their descendent is a distinct mutant—and a
prodigious one. 8,601 lines long and hence not much shorter
than Milton's *Paradise Lost* or Wordsworth's *Prelude*, it has the
effect of being a survey of humanity. Today it is read chiefly
by cultural historians as a source for knowledge of the England
of its day, but it as certainly deserves the attention of any poetry
reader who enjoys satire, psychological portraiture, narrative, or
description; Crabbe the moralist and Crabbe the artist keep
the long poem from being merely topical or simply catalogic.

Crabbe did not escape all pitfalls in a poem of such length
and scope. It suffers from unevenness of performance, and occasionally we suspect in its author a perverse tenacity in
accumulating enough material to cover a chosen subject, sufficient couplets to fill out a letter. This defect looms less large
than rumor has declared. Those who have not read *The Borough*
believe it to be a poem of *longueurs*; those who do read it,
and read it through, discover that nowhere does Crabbe utterly
fail. Out of such unlikely poetic subjects as sectarian controversy, the endowment and construction of a hospital, or the
tawdry lives of third-rate thespians he makes surprisingly much.
What sustains his verse when everything else—wit, pathos,
rhetoric, melody—appears to have flagged is an air of truth,
a gray unquenchable glow that gives his drabbest passages a
peculiar authority and that causes us to ponder once again on
the true relationship between truth, beauty, and poetry. As
we finish some passage which has nowhere impressed us, we
discover suddenly that each "limpid line" has been quietly
exerting its power all along.

It was Ezra Pound who applied the phrase "limpid line"
to Crabbe's poetry, allying him at the same time to Stendhal,
Browning, and Flaubert as Western literature's rediscoverers

of Dante's ability to keep the eye directly on the object. Pound's extravagant regard for Crabbe was such that he placed *The Borough* above anything by Wordsworth or Byron: "It at least shows a gleam of sense. The man *was* trying to put down things as they were . . . . He is in some ways more modern than a lot of moderns."[21]

An example of Crabbe's ability to creep up on us unseen is the passage telling why generations of lichens, ferns, and finally flowers have over the centuries luxuriated on the ancient stone of the borough church. The deceptively heavy-handed explanation of "Flora's triumph o'er the falling tower" turns out to have been a touching little poem on the paradoxes of mutability. Or consider the brazenly "unpoetic" couplets which tell how the unprincipled attorney Swallow used to disarm his friends with drink and meat while reducing them, as clients, to penury by pocketing their fortunes:

> His way to starve them was to make them eat,
> And drink oblivious draughts—to his applause
> It must be said, he never starved a cause;
> He'd roast and boil'd upon his board—the boast
> Of half his victims was his boil'd and roast—
> And these at every hour; he seldom took
> Aside his client, till he'd praised his cook;
> Nor to an office led him, there in pain
> To give his story and go out again,
> But first the brandy and the chine were seen,
> And then the business came by starts between.

Crabbe was seldom worse than this. Wit has declined into mere pun; the lines contain nothing remarkable rhetorically or structurally; and the diction is almost offensive. The pulse of poetry is beating weakly—yet it beats. Read in context, especially, the passage has a ring of truth to the fact that rises grimly clear above its deceptively banal orchestration.

Disturbed by complaints about *The Borough*, Crabbe spent most of his 1812 Preface to *Tales* defending himself as a realist and his verse as "poetry without an atmosphere," a phrase virtually coined by one of his critics. Crabbe was less realistic than he and his readers encouraged each other to think, but he did aim to see things as they are and to versify what he saw. By "atmosphere" Crabbe meant what his contemporaries called imaginative coloring, or what Wordsworth more beautifully called "the light that never was on sea or land." Crabbe's genius lies in the creation of another species of atmosphere: in catching some of the lights that, on land or sea, ever are—the abiding flavor, that is, of whatever subject matter he has picked. Two such verdicts as the critic Herford's and the poet Tennyson's are not incompatible. "Crabbe," said Tennyson, "has a world of his own," and only a few decades later Herford wrote that "the lustre of Scott's and Byron's tales is more tarnished than that of Crabbe's. The pageants of romance and of romantic history grow dim; the tragedy of everyday life always finds an echo and never loses its hold."[22]

Crabbe's poetry has, actually, a variety of atmospheres, all belonging to his world and colored by his temperament but evoking the variety of our own. Different indeed from the sinister banalities of the passage on Swallow are the details in the nostalgic dream of a prisoner in the letter on "Prisons." Sentenced to die and asleep in his cell, he recalls in a dream the innocence of his love for his sister and his betrothed, with whom he used to wander

> Through the green lane—then linger in the mead—
> Stray o'er the heath in all its purple bloom—
> And pluck the blossom where the wild bees hum;
> Then through the broomy bound with ease they pass,
> And press the sandy sheep-walk's slender grass,
> Where dwarfish flowers among the gorse are spread,
> And the lamb browses by the linnet's bed;
> Then 'cross the bounding brook they make their way
> O'er its rough bridge—and there behold the bay!—
> The ocean smiling to the fervid sun—
> The waves that faintly fall and slowly run—
> The ships at distance and the boats at hand;
> And now they walk upon the sea-side sand,
> Counting the number and what kind they be,
> Ships softly sinking in the sleepy sea.

In the cause of realism, Crabbe must be more ready to versify Swallow's mean tricks than lambs, linnets, and the sleepy sea—posing thereby an aesthetic problem for all his admirers, from Jeffrey on. Haddakin underlines the importance and thorniness of the problem by making it the central subject of her book on Crabbe, whose last chapter is entitled "Why not in Prose?"

Nearly all the unpoetical words, phrases, and verse paragraphs which have distressed Crabbe's readers are at least as defensible as Swallow's "boil'd and roast." A similar phrase in the eighteenth letter can quickly illustrate the point. In the atmospheric description of an odorous, unkempt tenement room shared by many families appears the infamous couplet "Each end contains a grate, and these beside/Are hung utensils for their boil'd and fried"—but this couplet better honors context than does the less objectionable, more Augustan one that soon follows: "There many a tea-cup's gaudy fragment stands,/All placed by vanity's unwearied hands . . . ."

The unlovely, precise language Crabbe employed as early as *The Village* ("rank weeds," "slimy mallow," "walls of mud," "naked rafters") and more freely in *The Borough* ("heaps of coal and coke," "old blue jacket," "dry shelly sand," "brick-floored parlour," "sun-burnt tar," "cards and cribbage-board") make him a pioneer in diction; his poetry is as much a criticism of the Neoclassical "inane phraseology," in particular the tinsel verbiage of Erasmus Darwin,[23] as Wordsworth's 1800 preface to the *Lyrical Ballads*. Crabbe's poetry actually surpasses Wordsworth's in employing what Wordsworth himself advised, "a selection of language really used by men"; but, because Crabbe does not often also "throw over" his subjects "a certain colouring of imagination, whereby ordinary things should be presented to the mind in unusual aspect," his lines can seem cumbersome or grotesque. They are so only if read without regard for the whole they are parts of. The following have been declared by a critic of Crabbe inexcusable:

His oxen low where monks retired to eat. . . . (*Bor.*, IV)

He sees . . . .
The house, the chamber, where he once array'd
His youthful person . . . . (*Bor.*, XXIII)

. . . he sometimes saved his cash,

By interlinear days of frugal hash. (*Tales*, V)

Thus extracted, they are inexcusable; but they should not have been extracted for display. Each belongs to a context which is the richer for its presence.

Crabbe's peculiar technical accomplishment as a poet is that, in retaining the heroic couplet, he put to new uses the native tendencies of a verse form that might have seemed too inflexible for his purposes. The couplet's epigrammatic tendency is narcissistic; the couplet aims to be poised, immaculate, self-regarding. It discourages complexities of context, and yet these we have been observing in excerpts from *The Register*. In *The Borough* Crabbe's couplets become yet less self-contained. Unlike the couplet in the hands of most Romantics, Crabbe's retains many technical characteristics of those of his original models—Pope and Dryden.[24] But they now achieve new effects—as when he tells us how a timid kind of love once briefly touched the lukewarm heart of the borough's vicar and

> led his patient spirit where it paid
> Its languid offerings to a listening maid;
> She, with her widow'd mother, heard him speak,
> And sought awhile to find what he would seek.
> Smiling he came, he smiled when he withdrew,
> And paid the same attention to the two;
> Meeting and parting without joy or pain,
> He seem'd to come that he might go again.

Our pleasure in these lines certainly involves their formal qualities as couplets, the balancings and antitheses. Yet our enjoyment of any single couplet or any device (such as the play upon *sought/seek* or the significant force allotted *come/go*) requires us to understand the situation and the vicar's character. Crabbe's couplets submit themselves always to the common good, the whole, whether it be a character drawing, a description, or a short story: "He stretched and adjusted the familiar couplet with singular address to his own purpose, nor has it ever again been used so well for that purpose . . . . It is not clear that 'Middlemarch,' cast into form like his, would not have had a better chance of performance. The narratives in blank verse of 'The Excursion' are more likely to be dull than Crabbe's heroics, to which dialogue and monologue are much better fitted."[25]

As much as he admired Crabbe, Byron feared that he had chosen a coarse, impracticable subject. Later schools of Realism and Naturalism have made Crabbe's subject seem less impracticable, and our current appetite for varieties of irony and innuendo has allowed a critic like Leavis to praise Crabbe by saying that his wit approaches that of the Metaphysical poets.[26] Certainly he seems more poetic today than he could have seemed to many Romantics and Victorians, who demanded either imagination's transfiguration of experience or the anodyne of rich music. Neither transfiguration nor rich musics does Crabbe generously provide. E. M. Forster has, however, rightly remarked that to be best appreciated Crabbe's poetry ought to be read aloud,[27] and *The Borough* itself begins with a descriptive letter more evocative than witty, emotional rather than ironic.

In the first half of this introductory "General Description," Crabbe appears to be organizing his letter by principle of contrast. He opposes borough scenes to the inland ones where his imagined correspondent lives. He manages thereby to subvert two impulses, and one of these is the impulse to make of this letter, once again, another *Village*. He early asks his correspondent why he might wish to turn his attention from the inland "winding streamlet, limpid, lingering, slow,/Where the reeds whisper when the zephyrs blow," to the borough's turbulent tidal river, the Alde, "strongest contrast to that stream" imaginable. Why should his friend, surrounded by country "beauty, lively or serene," wish to read of heath, bog, and spray-wet beach? As in *The Village*, Crabbe insists that the wildness which has certainly attracted him as a poet is repellent, and this he shall prove by unfavorable contrasting.

In *The Borough*, however, that other place is no longer assumed to be literary or imaginary. It is where his friend is. What are we to make, then, of these zephyrs and whispering reeds or of "village-pleasures unreproved by law," a "cheerful" sun, and happy deer? The place reminds us by day of Goldsmith but of Gray by twilight:

Gales from your jasmines soothe the evening gloom,
When from your upland paddock you look down,
And just perceive the smoke which hides the town;
When weary peasants at the close of day
Walk to their cots, and part upon the way;
When cattle slowly cross the shallow brook,
And shepherds pen their folds, and rest upon their crook.

The pastoral softness does not mean that Crabbe has capitulated,
but, like the better-humored side of *The Register,* it does signify
something of a truce. His antipathy to Aldeburgh has dwindled
in time, and his chaplaincy, curacy, and several livings in
Leicestershire and Lincolnshire have given him familiarity with
countrysides and townsfolk less blatantly unpastoral. In the
seventh of the tales he published in 1812, a wise widow urges
a fastidious young woman to abandon sentimental visions of
life and to accept overtures from a local peasant; and Crabbe
gives her an admonitory line that he himself has hearkened to:
"Think, I beseech you, better of the farm."

It was back in Suffolk, however, that Crabbe began work
on *The Borough.* The poem returns us to Aldeburgh and the
sea, both of which still aroused in Crabbe the impulse to
contrast unkindly. It is not irrelevant that our first glimpse of
the borough is of seaside stuff. Pleading that only the artist's
pencil may render streets and buildings, Crabbe deserts the un-
described town center for "half-buried buildings next the beach,"
where "squalid sea-dames" mend nets and their weary husbands
deposit their daily catch. Yet we stay with this cheerless scene
only a moment, for a restlessness pervades the letter's first half.
As if to escape the sea, we turn to the river. Being tidal, it
evokes what we have turned from:

With ceaseless motion comes and goes the tide,
Flowing, it fills the channel vast and wide;
Then back to sea, with strong majestic sweep
It rolls, in ebb yet terrible and deep;
Here sampire-banks and salt-wort bound the flood;
There stakes and sea-weeds withering on the mud;
And, higher up, a ridge of all things base,
Which some strong tide has roll'd upon the place.

Crabbe relates the atmosphere of these lines, as he had that of the landscape passage in *The Village,* to human experience. He places in his river scene the lone figure of a wet, cold oyster-dredger who,

> [his boat] driving with the tide,
> Beats his weak arms against his tarry side,
> Then drains the remnant of diluted gin . . . .

The sea, river, and marsh flats to which Crabbe allots three-quarters of his "General Description" are not described for their own sake, nor as simply a long poem's introductory frame establishing geographical limits. Wherever the borough's natural setting appears, it is presented as part of the human scene. Man and nature are uneasily but inextricably involved in each other:

> We prune our hedges, prime our slender trees,
> And nothing looks untutor'd and at ease;
> On the wide heath, or in the flow'ry vale,
> We scent the vapours of the sea-born gale;
> Broad-beaten paths lead on from stile to stile,
> And sewers from streets the road-side banks defile;
> Our guarded fields a sense of danger show,
> Where garden-crops with corn and clover grow;
> Fences are form'd of wreck and placed around
> (With tenters tipp'd), a strong repulsive bound;
> Wide and deep ditches by the gardens run,
> And there in ambush lie the trap and gun . . . .

Neither man's impingement on nature nor nature's on man is given greater emphasis, and man's on man is included as well. The sophistication of fences, which aim to make bad neighbors better, implies also the destructive power of nature; for the fences are fragments of men's ships which his neighbor ocean has crushed against her own coasts. Like the following letter's decaying church and forgotten generations of buried parishioners, the borough town seems fragile; it is impermanent next to the eternal ocean, whose waves gnaw forever at its edge, "Raking the rounded flints, which ages past/Roll'd by their rage, and shall to ages last." And the scent of sea water that unexpectedly blows in on the fourth line of the passage above may alert us to the fact that the dreadful sea, not man, has been allowed to dominate this letter.

Crabbe failed to subvert his second impulse, after all. The restlessness perceived earlier breaks forth in lines 163-270 as the surge of the sea. More than half of these many lines are somber—forty describe a winter storm upon the ocean; thirty-five, a shipwreck in that storm. The letter has submitted half-way through to the fascination of the dreadful element,

> Various and vast, sublime in all its forms,
> When lull'd by zephyrs, or when roused by storms,
> Its colours changing, when from clouds and sun
> Shades after shades upon the surface run;
> Embrown'd and horrid now, and now serene,
> In limpid blue, and evanescent green. . . .

Few of the saline airs circulating in this letter are dispersed by the three passages on the "social" pleasures of pubs and inns, and the beautiful description of the sea at summer noon cannot mitigate the prevailing atmosphere of gloom.

Unlike characters in eighteenth-century literature, Crabbe's characters rarely give the impression that they pass their lives in a world of rooms only, with a few brief excursions into neat garden or neighboring street. But neither do Crabbe's characters pass their lives in exhilarating harmony with the immensities of nature. He places his men and women geographically. We view them with some awareness of the sea that pounds, or shimmers, to the east, or of marshlands and fields to the southwest, sometimes of softer woods and vales; and this placement forces us always to remember that man and nature are mutually involved but not intermingled. Fitting it is that *The Borough*'s first letter is full of sea water, salty mud, and seamen. Later letters occasionally recall us to material with which the whole began—dramatically so in "Peter Grimes," "The Parish Clerk," and "Amusements" but less forcefully in such letters as "Elections" and "Inns." The "General Description" contributes to later letters a spirit of place. It also casts over them a philosophical coloring. Man, struggling with a natural world which alternately aids and ruins him, exhibits in himself her ambiguities, being now his own destroyer, now his own savior. What distinguishes man from the natural world is that, believing in what he has called good and evil, he is moral; she, apparently, is not. To Crabbe, nature can be more awesome than man; but she is seldom so interesting and, except as symbol, always less meaningful.

This distinction finds expression in the shipwreck which climaxes the first letter of *The Borough*. In a poem which insistently stoops to versifying such minutiae as the contents of a seaman's hut and varieties of seaweed, such mundane matters as a bawling baby's reactions to sleeping powders and a bill collector's airs, Crabbe makes an opening bid to qualify as a poet of what his age still called "the sublime." The largest aspects of nature were considered the most sublime, and in his handling of coast, night, sea, and storm he creates something of the mystery of the infinite or uncircumscribed, one of the required effects. As he builds towards his climax, Crabbe also keeps in mind the fact that his patron Burke's *Enquiry into the Sublime and Beautiful* (1757) had defined terror as a prime source of sublimity. Crabbe's sailormen and their wives have run down to the storm-darkened beach in a confusion of fragmented sights and sounds. Peering out now towards the battered, breaking ship, they can "discern/Lights, signs of terror, gleaming from the stern." Suddenly, though for only a few lines, the point of view effectively shifts from that of the helpless land-trapped onlookers to that of the sea-trapped sailors, who "view these lights upon the beach,/Which yield them hope, whom help can never reach." As suddenly, the horror of man's precarious position in nature is revealed to all:

> From parted clouds the moon her radiance throws
> On the wild waves, and all their danger shows;
> But shows them beaming in her shining vest,
> Terrific splendour! gloom in glory dress'd!
> This for a moment, and then clouds again
> Hide every beam, and fear and darkness reign.
>> But hear we now those sounds? Do lights appear?
> I see them not! the storm alone I hear:
> And lo! the sailors homeward take their way;
> Man must endure—let us submit and pray.

The sailors' deaths may have been meaningless. Moral man is a victim of the amoral physical world he must inhabit, and he is also its prisoner.

Crabbe cannot with certainty say that our sufferings at the hands of nature are wholly undeserved; he cannot with certainty say, either, that we wholly deserve the sufferings we bring upon ourselves. He is moved to deepest melancholy by those aspects of nature which imply her "hostility" to man: the uncontrollable sea, starved soil, or autumn, this last a reminder of the paradox that our vulnerable, mutable, and unruly bodies imprison the soul but give life to the mind and the senses. He feels more comfortable, therefore, contemplating the punishments for which we are apparently to blame than those for which we apparently are not.

The shipwreck over, he admits to relief that his general description is concluding. He attributes the relief to an aesthetic matter, his difficulty in handling description "of sea or river, of a quay or street," but it is nature's role in the letter that has really disturbed him. He looks forward to letters in which nature will resume a secondary role, promising us "happier" verse when he shifts his attention to "a happier theme" and subject—"Man . . . and the deeds of men." More congenial a subject than nature's amorality, more pleasing, is man's morality. Where a morality obtains, experience wears at least the garb of meaning. At the almost cheerful conclusion of the whole, dark-lit *Borough*, Crabbe recalls to us what his preferred subject has been, describing the poet, himself, as one who

> loves the mind in all its modes to trace,
> And all the manners of the changing race;
> Silent he walks the road of life along,
> And views the aims of its tumultuous throng;
> He finds what shapes the Proteus-passions take,
> And what strange waste of life and joy they make,
> And loves to show them in their varied ways,
> With honest blame or with unflattering praise.
> 'Tis good to know, 'tis pleasant to impart,
> These turns and movements of the human heart;
> The stronger features of the soul to paint,
> And make distinct the latent and the faint;

Man as he is, to place in all men's view. . . .

Gifford's complaint that Crabbe's poetry fails us "because it is precisely in order to escape from the world as it is, that we fly to poetry"[28] identifies more accurately the effect of *The Borough* than its poetic value. *The Borough* presses us towards life rather than releases us from it, and the poem's many thousand bits of realistic detail, its unpoetical diction, and its diversity of subject and character are consonant with Crabbe's aim to place in our view man as he is. How well did he impose upon all this material the order it should have as a coherent survey of the mind, manners, heart, and soul of that tumultuous throng, mankind?

Crabbe's son frankly declared that his father lacked in his poetry and in his life a sense of order. This "defect in his own mind"[29] was one Crabbe sometimes defended; in "The Learned Boy" (*Tales*, XXI) he remarks that "the love of order" finds its place "With all that's low, degrading, mean, and base" and that "love of method" is to many only an "armour and defence," something which "serves for lack of sense." *The Borough* does indeed have less order than we would wish— but more than was recognized by the *Monthly, Edinburgh,* and *Quarterly* reviews, whose sum verdict was that, because the poem lacks method and unity, it is an utterly confused production.

This leviathan of a poem has, however, submitted itself to half a dozen kinds of organization. All are imperfect, one is virtually negligible in effect, and the most effective ones are those least consciously conceived. The hopelessly arbitrary use of "letters" is but a pretense at organization, so irrelevant an imposition from without that after the first several hundred lines it becomes only an irritant. More authentic is the device, obliquely referred to in Crabbe's Preface, of grouping together persons or incidents that are related by subject or scene but, like the eccentric females of *The Register*, are distinguished by what Crabbe calls "many marks of discrimination." Good examples are letters XII through XVI ("Players," "The Alms-House and Trustees," and a letter for each of three inhabitants of the almshouse). The ways whereby this closely related sequence is unified are too various to explicate here. Simpler examples are letters II, III, and IV, which handle the borough church, two church officials, and the town's religious sects. The delicately managed love story which makes up the last of Letter II reads (like the sketch of a hospital governor many letters later) as if it had once been intended for *The Register*'s "Burials." But it is not a forced appendage to its letter. The church's graveyard serves as a satisfactory transition; melancholy and mutability relate it to what precedes, mutability and love to what follows, the sketch of the vicar.

Methods of organization less clearly conscious include the direction which *The Borough* seems to be taking as we move through it. Crabbe begins with the physical (letters I and II), shifts to the sociological (letters IV through XII), and moves on to the psychological (letters XIII through XXII)—in other terms, from the primarily descriptive through the primarily satirical towards the primarily narrative. Then, too, Crabbe's ubiquitous air of truth to fact colors the work and his "General Description" casts its own coloring forward over later letters. In the same manner Crabbe's moral intensity can become, as W. K. Thomas pointed out, a controlling force and principle of selection within any single letter dealing with diverse material.[30]

These several ways in which *The Borough* acquires a degree of unity still leave some questions practically unanswerable. Why, for example, is "Elections" placed between "Sects and Professions in Religion" and "Professions—Law"? Can it be simply the pleasures of the taproom that justifies placing "Inns" among letters on pastimes? Why does a poem which begins with the sea end with "Prisons" (XXIII) and "Schools" (XXIV)? To this third and most important question, however, we have a meaningful answer; but it is uncertain whether Crabbe himself would have given it. The poem's didactics announce and its characters' lives demonstrate that more men fail in life at some crucial level of responsibility than succeed. Their failure can be traced back to some weakness of character, and that character is usually revealed in early years. And, since punishment comes in the wake of that failure, *The Borough*'s moral tone and philosophic coloring find fit symbolic expression in

"Prisons" and "Schools." These two letters suggest, respectively, concluding and initial stages of moral experience; and the reversed chronology has its own point.

If the "dark and terrible pencil"[31] which sketched *The Borough* was guided by any single concept, it was of life as imprisonment; but the final letter's survey of schools and masters recalls us to the fact that not all men need be or are imprisoned. In childhood years "we find/The native bias of the opening mind." The bias can sometimes be checked, if dangerous; encouraged, if promising. And yet the preparatory school matron can but look sadly upon her erstwhile pupils grown into citizens, for few have allowed their native virtue to flourish and as few have kept their "latent evil" under rein.

The borough prison contains few villains. Crabbe's common sense told him, of course, that legal justice is imperfect, that law itself is highly fallible. Virtue may have to be its own reward, and life would be intolerable to contemplate if corporal imprisonment and execution were the only punishments for evil. The prison's criminals are a less villainous lot than the multitude never apprehended or convicted. The processes of punishment more often work themselves out in other ways. Like his suffering Jachin, Crabbe "saw/How much more fatal justice is than law." The dungeons into which most of his erring characters are cast are those of the self; in them, guilt-ridden visions harrow callous souls, like Grimes, or shame the tenderer ones. Hell or purgatory they suffer, depending on the crime.

In "Prisons" a literate debtor makes much of the resemblance between Homer's hell and the borough prison. Here, he says,

> we like ghosts and flitting shades appear:
> This is the hell he sings, and here we meet,
> And former deeds to new-made friends repeat;
> Heroic deeds, which here obtain us fame,
> And are in fact the causes why we came.
> Yes! this dim region is old Homer's hell,
> Abate but groves and meads of asphodel.

The tone darkens as the debtor, innocent in heart, says that this literal prison is a castle comparatively speaking; for "to the wretch whom care and guilt confound,/The world's a prison, with a wider bound . . . ." Crabbe's interest in close-focused views of nature lends itself to his portrayal of the prisons in which the multitude of criminals at large are confined. The scenery against which Keene, Jachin, and Grimes suffer their different kinds of punishment becomes a visualization of their punishment or of their suffering.

After Abel Keene's short-lived career as a gay blade has ground to its close, he suffers in the open air a solitary confinement:

> we saw him on the beach reclined,
> Or causeless walking in the wint'ry wind;
> And, when it raised a loud and angry sea,
> He stood and gazed, in wretched reverie;
> He heeded not the frost, the rain, the snow;
> Close by the sea he walk'd alone and slow.
> Sometimes his frame through many an hour he spread
> Upon a tombstone, moveless as the dead;
> And, was there found a sad and silent place,
> There would he creep with slow and measured pace.
> Then would he wander by the river's side,
> And fix his eyes upon the falling tide;
> The deep dry ditch, the rushes in the fen,
> And mossy crag-pits were his lodgings then:
> There, to his discontented thoughts a prey,
> The melancholy mortal pined away.

We are first shown Abel wandering amidst the greater and also more alien aspects of nature, cut off from humanity and thus from meaning. Then, as the setting, that "wider bound," contracts and we for a moment see him as an effigy upon a gravestone, the sense of his hopeless imprisonment increases. His imminent death by suicide is appropriately more violent than the death of Jachin, a gentler, less heinous offender. When Jachin's long-successful ruse of dropping collection money into his bran-lined pocket has been exposed, he faints away from shame, enduring, without so much as a groan, "A death-wound never to be heal'd." After a period of exile like Keene's, he quietly turns his face to the wall in an abandoned loft and dies.

The death of Grimes, the true villain of the three, is the

most turbulent and gruesome. His monologue as death approaches alludes, like that of Dr. Faustus, to the devils that are after him. Unlike Faustus, Grimes has been delivered up long before to a posse of tormentors. During his last year he might at any hour well have exclaimed, with Mephistopheles this time, "Why, this is hell, nor am I out of it." The spirits of his dead father, whom he once felled in anger, and of his three apprentices, dead in his employ, took to haunting the river where he fished for his livelihood:

> I saw my father on the water stand,
> And hold a thin pale boy in either hand;
> And there they glided ghastly on the top
> Of the salt flood, and never touch'd a drop.
> I would have struck them, but they knew th' intent,
> And smiled upon the oar, and down they went.

Later they become bolder, taunt him, and with "weak, sad" cries of "Come, come" bid him leap to his death. Finally "the demons" drive him insane by flinging in his face handfuls of salt water mixed with blood and fire. "The heart of man," wrote Sir Thomas Browne in *Religio Medici*, "is the place the Devils dwell in: I feel sometimes a Hell within my self; Lucifer keeps his Court in my breast, Legion is revived in me . . . ." Peter Grimes's own misdeeds had established the necessity for the apparitions that punish him, and their particular forms and actions Peter himself conceived. And now, perhaps, Peter will sleep the sleep of clay—"For what has death in any form to give," Crabbe asks in the less lurid letter on Jachin, "Equal to that man's terrors, if he live?"

More lurid yet and more melodramatic is "Ellen Orford" (Letter XX), though her claims to innocence would surpass Jachin's. One of the reasons Crabbe treats Ellen and her sons so harshly is that in *The Borough* he has not yet outgrown his early impression that poverty and evil are mutually involved. L. J. Wylie observed that among the more prosperous characters of Crabbe's late tales "The ravages of evil are none the less evident because the subtler self-seeking depicted in them seems at first glance utterly trivial, or because the wrongdoer escapes the merely physical punishment that is his due."[32]

This observation needs qualification. Even at the level of the "merely physical," Ellen Orford, like certain other of Crabbe's figures, receives punishment so far beyond her due that the effect is closer to bathos than to pathos. Crabbe never wholly rid himself of the suspicion that the wages of sin may well be penury. "Will you embrace contempt and beggary?" an angry father in "The Widow's Tale" (*Tales,* VII) asks a daughter whom he has just realized is "wandering o'er enchanted ground"—is recklessly in love.

> " 'Can you endure to see each other cursed
> By want, of every human wo the worst?
> Warring for ever with distress, in dread
> Either of begging or of wanting bread;
> While poverty, with unrelenting force,
> Will your own offspring from your love divorce . . . ?' "

The terrors of a fall into poverty, much greater in Crabbe's day than in ours, makes such a fall a powerful moral metaphor intended to encourage us to believe that some system of significant merits and demerits does exist. Even in *Tales of the Hall* (1819), we may occasionally receive the impression that poverty is not only a root of evil but one of its flowers, especially in the twelfth book, "Sir Owen Dale," for which, as we shall later see, Crabbe once again borrowed remembered terrors of Aldeburgh's poverty to impress us with the terrors of spiritual poverty. This is what he did in "Ellen Orford." Ellen does not really belong with the company she keeps in the last third of *The Borough*—Abel Keene, Jachin, Peter Grimes, or the masterfully conceived and sketched Sir Denys Brand. She more resembles Hester of the 1804 ballad, for both women were seduced and deserted by men high above them in station, both consequently suffered dreadful degradation, and both survived to tell the tale in person.

The long, entertaining prelude on novels which Crabbe affixes to "Ellen Orford" has as its theme the discrepancy between literature and life—a genial rehandling of *The Village*'s main theme. For Crabbe, the physical is still more tangible than the psychical, and its details seem easier to corroborate, so *The Borough*, produced by a poet not yet fully matured, too readily

employs pictures of physical wretchedness to illustrate in concrete images the citizens' mental or emotional frailties. "Ellen
Orford" is the grotesque prime example, the giveaway. Her
downward plunge belongs with those simply less bathetic de-
clines of the profligate actor Frederic Thompson and Sir Denys'
favored but sinful trio of the almshouse. This almshouse is another image of incarceration and as such joins the prison and
schools of the last books, the natural world of the first, the cruel-
ly cabined souls of many books, and the borough itself—man's
world in gloomy miniature.

In *The Borough,* we are best able to respond to incarceration
imaged by natural setting—the device is subtle, the final
effect is not that of caricature, and Crabbe's partiality for
minute description of the out-of-doors results in tints and tones
whose delicacy contradicts the legend of the harsh, bludgeoning
Crabbe. Some significant differences between Crabbe's frequent use of "emotional" setting and his predecessors' infrequent
use of it may be seen through a comparison. The distraught lover
in a poem by an earlier and more famous poet tells her beloved, to whom she is writing a letter, that her recently re-
awakened anguish over their separation has destroyed the
restorative powers of a landscape long familiar to her:

> No more these scenes my meditation aid,
> Nor lull to rest the visionary maid:
> But o'er the twilight groves and dusky caves,
> Long-sounding aisles and intermingled graves,
> Black Melancholy sits, and round her throws
> A death-like silence, and a dread repose:
> Her gloomy presence saddens all the scene,
> Shades every flower, and darkens every green,
> Deepens the murmur of the falling floods,
> And breathes a browner horror on the woods.

The power which this seated figure, Melancholy, has of shading
the colors of flower and wood derives from the feelings of
the observer, who happens to be Pope's Eloisa writing to her
Abelard. Melancholy is a personification of the Romantics' shaping power of the imagination; her seat really lies, like the brown
horror of those woods, not outside Eloisa but within. Pope is

nearly "Romantic" here, but his brooding woman sits at an un-Romantic distance from her landscape, an aesthetic spectator, as it were, or the conscious letter writer she actually is; and from there she observes the nicely framed vista that her spirits have decorously embrowned and her pen as decorously reproduces.

In contrast, neither Crabbe nor his brooding Peter Grimes envisages a personification, and Grimes is wholly immersed in his sceneries, almost himself the genius of the place:

> When tides were neap, and, in the sultry day,
> Through the tall bounding mud-banks made their way,
> Which on each side rose swelling, and below
> The dark warm flood ran silently and slow:
> There anchoring, Peter chose from man to hide,
> There hang his head, and view the lazy tide
> In its hot slimy channel slowly glide;
> Where the small eels that left the deeper way
> For the warm shore, within the shallows play;
> Where gaping muscles, left upon the mud,
> Slope their slow passage to the fallen flood:—
> Here dull and hopeless he'd lie down and trace
> How sidelong crabs had scrawl'd their crooked race;
> Or sadly listen to the tuneless cry
> Of fishing gull or clanging golden-eye. . . .

Like the unusual diction and music of these lines, the details of Grimes's even "browner horror" as he succumbs to a murderer's neuroses could not be mistaken for Eloisa's elegantly darkening landscape. Her abstract genius does not quite make the shift from Miltonic to Romantic melancholy. Crabbe's passage could not, in fact, be mistaken for any setting out of eighteenth-century poetry.

Crabbe's fame has lain in his having versified the lives of the poor. He is a greater poet, however, when he borrows from Aldeburgh its landscape than when he depicts its poorhouse. Neither kind of setting figures so importantly in his masterworks, *Tales* and *Tales of the Hall*, but he used both kinds frequently in *The Borough* as graphic means of showing us man as, Crabbe then thought, he is: a creature in whom evil, as ubiquitous as poverty, heavily outweighs the good with which it is mixed, a creature at the mercy of nature and nearly doomed by his own natural weakness. A half dozen figures illustrate that such a doom need not be total or final, and Ellen Orford is among them. Her determination, once she has fallen, is to achieve serenity through atonement and resignation. She succeeds. Her success makes Crabbe happy—we remember that man's capabilities for willing good helped Crabbe love "the mind in all its modes to trace." Although there is a streak of fatalism in Crabbe—as, it would seem, there must be in all realistic appraisals of life—his tales of 1812 and especially of 1819 allow for an even greater magnification of free will than More allowed him. Ellen's terrible life, that grotesque exercise in expressionism, should have been passed in the hopeless abysm where the 1783 village lies. But in spirit and accomplishment she herself belongs, unlike Hester, among the wiser ones of the later tales.

CHAPTER 4

Fulfillments

I *Neither Mad nor Mean*

FOR some years after the publication of the 1812 *Tales in Verse*, Crabbe enjoyed a popularity surpassed only by Scott, Moore, and, eventually, Byron. The fact that first editions of his nineteenth-century productions were, until a few decades ago, available in quantity in England's secondhand bookstores points both to the esteem Crabbe once enjoyed and to the century-long disesteem into which he rather abruptly fell. In 1818 the publisher Murray offered and paid three thousand pounds for the copyright of his works, including *Tales of the Hall*, which was to be published the next year. Although Moore had received in 1816 the same amount for *Lalla Rookh* alone, this was an impressive sum. Crabbe was delighted and so, apparently, was Murray. Nevertheless, Crabbe's reputation may have been in the descendency before the bargain was struck. *Tales of the Hall* went into a second edition within a year of its publication, but its sales were disappointing. By 1825 Wordsworth was able to speculate, with a touch of self-congratulation, on Crabbe's "want of popularity."[1] Crabbe's brief reign as England's most arresting "new" poet is one of the more curious phenomena of that decade. To understand it, we must consider what kind of poet he was, what kind of poetry he wrote, and what kinds of audience he reached.

To begin with, the sheer bulk of the poetry he made available between 1807 and 1812 was noteworthy: in six years, three volumes of heroic couplets, two of which would be called voluminous by any standards. His unexpected reappearance upon the literary scene after so long an absence had a double effect. It awakened a long-slumbering interest among those who had read his *Village* a quarter of a century earlier, and it aroused the curiosity of a new generation which had been in its cradles when that moderately renowned poem had appeared.

Crabbe's independence in choice of subject matter and in kinds of emphasis captured for a while the affections of the avant-garde. Sensitive to changing winds and responding as the young usually do to contemporary explorations among the arts, they admired in Crabbe's recent work signs of experimentation and self-reliance. An oddly dated member of the avant-garde he surely was, but some of those "young men" whom Coleridge claimed had read Wordsworth with full sympathy from the very beginning[2] were reading old Crabbe with sympathy too. In various quarters he was hailed as "an *original* poet"; in particular, as "the most original poet that ever sang of country life and manners"; in short, as "one of the most original poets of the present century."[3] The parents of those who found Crabbe so daring, even iconoclastic, admired him for quite other reasons. If confused or outraged by "modern" poetry, they could turn to Crabbe for reassurance. Poetically, morally, temperamentally, he seemed to represent for them the stability, even the sanity, of a rapidly vanishing age. So, on the one hand, the conservative Jeffrey could brandish Crabbe as a weapon in his war against the half-mad "lakers"; on the other hand, the notorious Caroline Lamb, as mercurial as Shelley and as morally quixotic as Byron, could wish to make the white-haired poet her personal adviser. What an extraordinary liaison *that* would have been—but Crabbe, of course, evaded her.[4]

He was doomed to lose both species of admirers. The older generation, its taste formed forty or fifty years earlier, was dying off, and his younger readers were beginning to discover elsewhere work more surely to their liking. Before 1807, the year of Crabbe's *Poems*, no single Romantic—not Coleridge or Wordsworth, Blake or Burns—had yet attracted wide attention; and by 1812, the year of *Tales in Verse*, not much had been added to the Romantics' repertoire—Scott's *Marmion* and *Lady of the Lake*, Byron's *English Bards*, some early work by Shelley. In 1814 Crabbe's *Tales* went into its fifth edition. But in 1812 appeared the first two cantos of *Childe Harold*, and it was as if the Childe had raised a cry to arms. Between then and 1819, Byron himself published great quantities of verse, much of it narrative, including the rest of *Childe Harold* and *Beppo*, so that when Murray published the first two cantos of *Don Juan* in 1819, Byron's popularity was already legendary.

This was the year of *Tales of the Hall*, which now had to compete also with nine of Scott's Waverley novels and with much of his verse; Shelley's *Queen Mab, Alastor,* and *The Revolt of Islam;* Wordsworth's *Excursion, White Doe of Rylstone,* a two-volume reissue of lyrics, *Peter Bell* and *The Waggoner;* and even with Keats's *Poems* and *Endymion.* Only some of these works found an eager public, of course, nor had Hazlitt, defender of the new writers, yet been able to depose Jeffrey from the throne of criticism. But, even with most of the influential reviews supporting him, Crabbe could not long retain his position.

If Benjamin Britten's opera *Peter Grimes* were strictly faithful to its sources in *The Borough,* we would have to call Crabbe a High Romantic. He certainly is not that. Neither is he the High Augustan that a hasty contrast with Coleridge or Shelley might suggest. To what degree Crabbe belongs to either of the periods in which he attracted considerable attention has been a side issue in most studies of Crabbe—as it has been, in fact, in the preceding chapters of this one. We ought now to turn directly to the matter.

Henri Peyre has pointed out that Crabbe's English contemporaries, the prominent members of the generation approaching manhood about 1770, are Bentham, Godwin, Mary Wollstonecraft, Cobbett, Chatterton, Blake, Burns, Sheridan, Dugald Stewart, Beckford, and Joanna Baillie.[5] Among this Janus-faced family Crabbe is rather at home. Although unable, finally, to compete with the rising Romantics, Crabbe had come of age in that curious period usually called either post-Augustan or pre-Romantic. The period's sensibilities influenced Crabbe; his helped shape those of the young Romantics; and theirs, in turn, touched his.

Crabbe's native melancholy strain, augmented by an early familiarity with Young,[6] is not far distant from the melancholies of young Goethe, de Vigny, or Byron. F. L. Lucas sees Crabbe as an impressive member of the Graveyard School, and as a more successful practitioner, when so inclined, than Gray himself; Geoffrey Grigson sees evidence of a Romantic Crabbe when Coleridge was only seven years old and Wordsworth nine, observing, for example, that in a 1779 fragment Crabbe wrote, "Still I pass on, and now before me find/The restless ocean, emblem of my mind . . . ."[7] And as for that "Byronic mock-innocence" which W. K. Thomas discovers in some of Crabbe, Shaw's description in *Arms and the Man* of Sergius' postwar Byronism might well have been written to describe Crabbe as he affected many contemporary readers: "he has acquired the half tragic, half ironic air, the mysterious moodiness, the suggestion of a strange and terrible history . . . ."

As a boy, Crabbe had so nourished his impressionable mind on romances and Gothic novels that a poetaster complaining in 1818 that Byron's muse had turned impure, "Gathering poor scraps, that Coleridge might refuse,/From Gothic wastes—where Crabbe at length has rov'd," may well have been thinking not simply of Crabbe's few "wild" ballads, like "Sir Eustace," but of certain sensational parts of *The Borough*.[8] Over three decades, Crabbe turned periodically to the writing of ghost tales, dream poems, and vision poems; but he published fewer than he withheld. The *Lyrical Ballads* may have had, therefore, a greater influence on Crabbe than the less representatively Romantic narratives of Scott or Byron.[9] In the opening of the fifth tale of *Tales in Verse* is cataloged the reading material of the child John, the poem's unfortunate hero, who suffers deeply in maturity for having indulged his visionary schemes:

> doleful ballads, songs
> Of lovers' sufferings and of ladies' wrongs;
> Of peevish ghosts who came at dark midnight,
> For breach of promise guilty men to fright;
> Love, marriage, murder were the themes, with these,
> All that on idle ardent spirits seize. . . .

Such was the reading material of that seldom idle but ardent child George Crabbe, and such is the stuff of many of his tales.

Literature of sentiment left as sure a mark upon him as sensational literature, to which it is allied. When a central character of *Tales of the Hall* traces the growth of his naturally poetic mind, he includes references to novels that remind us of Crabbe's ambivalence on the subject in *The Library*:

> "Then was I pleased in lonely ways to tread,
> And muse on tragic tales of lovers dead;
> For all the merit I could then descry
> In man or woman was for love to die.
> I mused on charmers chaste, who pledged their truth,
> And left no more the once-accepted youth;
> Though he disloyal, lost, diseased, became,
> The widow'd turtle's was a deathless flame.
> This faith, this feeling, gave my soul delight:
> Truth in the lady, ardour in the knight. . . ."

The synopses of some of Crabbe's tales are chastened versions of this passage, whose third and fourth lines surely allude to the most famous play by Crabbe's beloved Dryden. Among the sentimental ingredients of *All for Love,* one of the grander fathers of eighteenth-century sentimentalism, is the un-Roman sensibility of Antony's soulmate, Dolabella:

> Nature has cast me in so soft a mould,
> That but to hear a story, feigned for pleasure,
> Of some sad lover's death, moistens my eyes,
> And robs me of my manhood.

Although a greater number of Crabbe's tales are clothed in disenchantment, the clothing does not fully hide the bones of the sentimental or romantic beneath. For instance, in "The Parting Hour" (*Tales,* II) the deserted Judith, who does marry but marries unhappily, nurtures for forty years the flame of her allegiance to her deserter, Allen; and he, disloyal, lost, diseased, returns finally to die in her arms. It is in Tennyson's famous "Enoch Arden," a lushly ornamented rehandling of this poem, that the innate sentimentality of the tale opens to full bloom. Under Crabbe's firmer treatment, the tale's ironies achieve a genuinely Romantic power.

To the literature of sentiment, of the Gothic novel, and of Young may be added other influences upon Crabbe which we usually consider influences upon the Romantics. There is, for example, the landscape school of the "picturesque," which traverses the eighteenth century, gathering momentum and depth as it goes, and to which Crabbe contributed as distinctly as any Romantic. In turning scientific knowledge to poetic uses, Crabbe early in his career gave a foretaste of that reunion of natural history and poetry which was later to attract young Coleridge even to Darwin's poetically grotesque *Loves of the Plants*—and was, as well, to become one of Wordsworth's declared aims.[10] *The Village*'s preoccupation with the poor peasants and their countryside betrays little of that kind of sympathy we call Rousseauistic, but it helped arouse poets to the poetic possibilities in humble, familiar things.

Crabbe was a pressure at work upon both Wordsworth and Coleridge as theorists. Since he was considered "one of the most original poets of the present century," he presented a peculiar problem. Describing nature from firsthand observation, he used, characteristically, an uninflated and unornamented vocabulary. He chose the common man, especially when poor or outcast, as his favorite character. He helped relocate forever the sources of English poetry closer to everyday experience. Such properties of Crabbe's verse Wordsworth and Coleridge at one time or another declared to be among the properties of their own. Crabbe's Dutch paintings in heroics forced Wordsworth and Coleridge to refine their aesthetics so as to exclude Crabbe's poetry, which neither would confess to enjoying. Their displeasure over a poet who held little respect for imagination and who employed couplets for nearly all his purposes was increased by the apparent ease with which Crabbe had achieved his position as a poetic luminary during the very years they were vainly struggling for proper recognition.

Hazlitt remarked that Wordsworth's failure to become early a popular poet had made him "apt to grudge and cavil at every particle of praise bestowed" on poets he felt superior to: "Mr. Wordsworth has thought too much of contemporary critics and criticism . . . ."[11] One of the aims of Wordsworth's Preface of 1815 was to discredit the aesthetics of the inimical Jeffrey, and this involved discrediting the poetry of Jeffrey's useful and enviably popular Crabbe. Not mentioned in the Preface, Crabbe was nevertheless in Wordsworth's mind even as he composed the opening paragraph. The least important of the six "powers requisite for the production of poetry," wrote Wordsworth, is fidelity of description—exactly what Crabbe was most frequently admired for. Wordsworth admitted that it was a power "indispensable" to the poet, but he argued that it ought only occasionally to be employed since "its exercise supposes all the higher qualities of the mind to be passive, and in a state of subjection to external objects, much in the same way as a translator or engraver ought to be to his original." The allusion to engraving would have brought Crabbe to the mind of most of Wordsworth's 1815 readers. Seven years before, Wordsworth had complained to Rogers that "nineteen out of twenty of Crabbe's pictures are mere matters of fact, with which the muses have just about as much to do as they have with a collection of medical reports . . . ."[12]

The shadow of Crabbe lies also on certain pages of the *Biographia Literaria*, published in 1817. Of the five "defects" which Coleridge identifies in Wordsworth's poetry, four are characteristics of Crabbe's verse; and the defect which he treats twice as lengthily as the other four together includes aspects of Crabbe's verse which had established his fame: a "minute adherence to *matter-of-fact* in character and incidents; a *biographical* attention to probability, and an anxiety of explanation . . . ." The greatest of Wordsworth's powers, Coleridge explains, is the power of imagination; he elsewhere identifies as Crabbe's essential failure "an absolute defect of high imagination; he gives me little or no pleasure: yet," he loftily continues, from the secure vantage point of 1834, "no doubt, he has much power of a certain kind, and it is good to cultivate, even at some pains, a catholic taste in literature."[13]

Crabbe early realized, as the Romantics came to discover, that within the familiar, the mundane, lay often the germs of the marvelous. He shared with his audience a fascination for the eccentric, the extraordinary, even for psychological extremes —whatever, in short, existed he considered a fit subject for poetry. This is a kind of Romantic doctrine of plenitude, and the Preface to *The Borough* shows that Crabbe was quite aware of his own iconoclasm in believing that whatever in life is, in art can be interesting. His fascination for the extraordinary led him to tell Scott in 1812 or 1813 that he had long desired

to turn his attention to the study of law reports, which then
seemed to be occupying Scott "—that is, brief histories of extraordinary cases, with the judgments. If that is what is meant
by *reports,* such reading must be pleasant . . . ."[14] By careful
attention to the psychological processes which produce and
are caused by men's actions, Crabbe makes extraordinary material out of so unsensational a matter as the impulse which
one day turns Jachin, the vicar's clerk, to petty thievery
(*Borough,* XIX), or the vicious maternal vanity that makes
of a plain but healthy girl a religious psychopath (*Tales,* VIII),
or that sympathy between male pupil and female tutor which
leads to a denouement infected by hints of incest and the
supernatural (*Tales of the Hall,* XVI).

Crabbe has been compared to an astonishing variety of his
contemporaries—to Wordsworth for several obvious reasons, but
also to Blake, Burns, Byron, Chatterton, Keats, Scott, Shelley.
Walter Broman has noted, for example, that in *The Borough*
the "smell of tar and weeds" is "certainly as vivid as the scents
of Keats"; and, although analogies between Crabbe and Keats
may seem stretched, Oliver Elton also sensed a kinship, won-
dering whether Keats aided Crabbe to escape yet "more
thoroughly" from the control of Augustan poetry, for "we could
almost believe that some lines Crabbe wrote in 1817 or 1818
were shaped after reading Keats, whose 'Endymion' came out
in the spring of the latter year."[15] Of one of the autobiographical
figures in *Tales of the Hall,* Edward Thomas asked: "What
would such a boy have grown to be had he lived as delicately
as Shelley?" Coventry Patmore insisted that Crabbe and Shelley
were utterly antipodal types, in taste, morality, religion, sensitivity, language, and even sexual orientation; but Thomas'
unanswerable question is meaningful if, remembering that Shel-
leyan visitation of Inspiration rapturously described in the
early *Candidate,* we read the 1819 lines of Crabbe that Thomas
had particularly in mind:

> "I loved to walk where none had walk'd before,
> About the rocks that ran along the shore;
> Or far beyond the sight of men to stray,
> And take my pleasure when I lost my way;
> For then 'twas mine to trace the hilly heath,

And all the mossy moor that lies beneath:
Here had I favourite stations, where I stood
And heard the murmurs of the ocean-flood,
With not a sound beside, except when flew
Aloft the lapwing, or the gray curlew,
Who with wild notes my fancied power defied,
And mock'd the dreams of solitary pride. . . ."

The more striking parallel is with Byron, who nearly a decade before had published in *Childe Harold* such a stanza as that beginning:

To sit on rocks, to muse o'er flood and fell,
To slowly trace the forest's shady scene,
Where things that own not man's dominion dwell,
And mortal foot hath ne'er or rarely been. . . .

Penned by "the last Augustan" in his sixties, Crabbe's lines touch upon major Romantic themes: wild nature (both land and sea), solitude, the appeal of the unregulated (that otherwise Augustan line "And take my pleasure when I lost my way"), the supremacy of self, the poignancy of the gulf between man and nature, and even that kind of irony we call Romantic, for the passage is critical of the emotional experiences whose recollection its author cherishes. Generally Crabbe was critical of the Romantics as practical moralists, as when he alludes bitterly (*Posthumous Tales, III*) to Keats's Grecian Urn ode in reviewing the collapse into marital wretchedness suffered by a couple who once pursued each other pantingly: "Oh! happy, happy, happy pair! both sought,/Both seeking—catching both, and caught!"; or when he writes, in obvious allusion to Wordsworth, that "Comfort grows not always by the Rills,/By running Brooks or dancing Daffodils . . . ."[16] However, Wordsworth, like Keats, may have been one of the modifiers of Crabbe's style and tone. As first described, Rachel of "Smugglers and Poachers" (*Tales of the Hall,* XXI) is Wordsworth's Lucy filtered through an elder sensibility. Crabbe's cottage-girl is a

child of gracious nature, ever neat
And never fine; a flow'ret simply sweet,
Seeming at least unconscious she was fair;

> Meek in her spirit, timid in her air,
> And shrinking from his glance if one presumed
> To come too near the beauty as it bloom'd.

Whitehead has pointed out, cautiously, "the suggestion of Wordsworthian influence" here and there throughout "Silford Hall" (*Posthumous Tales,* I).[17]

A striking philosophical affinity between Crabbe and some of the Romantics is Crabbe's perception of the relationships among the mind, the external world, and art. When Crabbe defends his transcription of life's distresses by declaring that his intention is to dissipate his reader's distress, he is basing his defense on an aesthetic which inverts rather than contradicts a Romantic one. After expressing the hope, in his Preface to the *Tales,* that his narratives will engage his reader's interest but "possess not interest sufficient to create painful sensations," Crabbe adds: "Fiction itself, we know, and every work of fancy, must for a time have the effect of realities . . . in truth, I can but consider this pleasant effect upon the mind of a reader as depending neither upon the events related (whether they be actual or imaginary), nor upon the characters introduced (whether taken from life or fancy), but upon the manner in which the poem itself is conducted."

His poetry's events and characters were, indeed, nearly always modeled directly after life. They are frequently painful ones, but their effect is to be "pleasant," for they shall, he had announced in *The Library,* "lead us willing from ourselves, to see/Others more wretched, more undone than we . . . ." The presence of the word *willing* suggests a curious analogy between Crabbe's remarks and Coleridge's famous phrase of decades later. Crabbe's readers are asked to suspend their disbelief in order to accept, not the imaginary as real, but the real as imaginary. The poet can give an air of romance to realities which resemble "the very concerns and distresses of the reader," the 1812 Preface continues, "for, when it is admitted that they have no particular relation to him, but are the troubles and anxieties of other men, they excite and interest his feelings as the imaginary exploits, adventures, and perils of romance . . . ." If Crabbe is to be taken at his word, he considered himself a writer of Romance after all, one who transformed reality even while focusing upon it.

It is probable that Coleridge's "Ancient Mariner" influenced Crabbe's handling of the favorite themes of pursuit and guilt in "The World of Dreams."[18] Even more probable is it that Coleridge's Dejection ode, first printed in 1802, contributed to the composition of lines in the tenth story of *Tales*, "The Lover's Journey," a poem which states what Coleridge had stated and what Locke, before him, had implied: the "'mind is incorrigibly poetical.'"[19] Crabbe rarely suggested relativism so baldly as in a line in the undated but probably early lyric "Revival": "It is the Mind that makes the Truth." Indeed, when he writes in "Lady Barbara" (*Tales of the Hall*, XVI) that "some strong passion's troubled reign" can turn an "outward object" into an inward, unreal vision as convincing as its source, his aim is to mock all seers of ghosts—as well as, perhaps, the more visionary of the seers of Parnassus. But in the opening lines of "The Lover's Journey," his aim is not to disabuse but to explain:

> It is the soul that sees; the outward eyes
> Present the object, but the mind descries;
> And thence delight, disgust, or cool indiff'rence rise:
> When minds are joyful, then we look around,
> And what is seen is all on fairy ground;
> Again they sicken, and on every view
> Cast their own dull and melancholy hue;
> Or, if absorb'd by their peculiar cares,
> The vacant eye on viewless matter glares,
> Our feelings still upon our views attend,
> And their own natures to the objects lend;
> Sorrow and joy are in their influence sure,
> Long as the passion reigns th' effects endure;
> But love in minds his various changes makes,
> And clothes each object with the change he takes;
> His light and shade on every view he throws,
> And on each object, what he feels, bestows.

Crabbe had already consciously put this theory into practice in *The Borough* and perhaps unconsciously in passages of *The Village*.

He could have seen only nonsense in a suggestion like Wordsworth's that moral wisdom can pulse towards us from a landscape. Crabbe's interest is in the reverse process; the mind's ability to impose itself or its coloring upon the outer world. Nevertheless, he mistrusted not only the powerful dejection Coleridge deplores in his ode but also the inspiring joy Coleridge finds so blessed. Either condition is an emotional extreme; either breeds, therefore, the illusions that lead to delusion. The lines from "The Lover's Journey," a poem based upon journeys that Crabbe made in 1778 or 1779 between Aldeburgh and Beccles as a lover courting his fiancée, contain clues to the important divergence between Crabbe's view and Coleridge's. Like "joy," which plays an important part in both poems, the word "joyful" is in Crabbe's poem allied to "fairy ground," a phrase which as early as *The Library* had become an allusion to danger. The pungent verb "sicken" keeps our attention on the unhealthiness of extremes, and "Again" certainly means more than "and now." The concluding couplets restate Crabbe's point that our perception of external reality is at the mercy of passions in themselves less than trustworthy.

Upon this emphasis the poem also ends. Orlando, the lover, has experienced the first two states of illusion, delight and disgust; and he is now experiencing the third, indifference. He had found an unlovely landscape beautiful during his horse-back journey towards his Laura—love's joy had been casting its enchantment upon reality. The second stage of his journey had come when he learned that Laura had gone off on a visit to "a friend," whom he at once assumes to be a rival. Now the dejected lover has followed after, riding through beautiful sceneries which impress him as ugly, vile—love's dejection has cast over reality its peculiar veil. When, however, Orlando is reunited to his faithful Laura (the friend was female) and they are riding happily back to her home, he is wholly oblivious to the beauty he had found ugly the day before; and, as he returns alone to his own home the next day, he is just as oblivious, lost in love dreams, to the ugliness he had found beautiful. The poem's concluding lines allude directly to Coleridge's ode:

Then could these scenes the former joys renew?

Or was there now dejection in the view?—
Nor one or other would they yield—and why?
The mind was absent, and the vacant eye
Wander'd o'er viewless scenes, that but appear'd to die.

Identifying intense joy and dejection as equally specious and
adding a third illusory state besides, Crabbe's poem reminds
us that part of his popularity lay in his vestigal Augustanism.
Hazlitt declared that passion speaks truer than reason; Crabbe
declares the reverse, but his conviction, though deep rooted, is
seldom complacently illustrated and often lies submerged in
the 1812 *Tales*. Whether on the surface or submerged, it gives
the *Tales* its special cast.

It was his preference for heroic couplets, his rather bitter
realism, and his melancholy that made Crabbe one of Byron's
favorite poets—amphibious Byron, who really felt more at home
on the *terra firma* of Neoclassicism than in the Romantic sea.
It was more than whimsical humor that led cautious, "reasonable"
Jane Austen to call Crabbe the most marriageable man of the
age. Crabbe was Scott's favorite poet, too, but Scott is no more
a full-fledged Romantic than Byron or Austen.

Because the Augustan appeals in Crabbe's work are simpler
to enumerate and define, they have been more often examined
than have the Romantic ones. Readers of our day whose inclination is to dissociate Crabbe from the Romantic movement
include Peter Quennell, Philip Henderson, Varley Lang, Arthur
Sale, W. K. Thomas, and Frank Whitehead; the most sustained
of these attempts lies in the introduction and notes to Whitehead's *Selections*. The same year *Tales of the Hall* appeared,
C. H. Terrot, a conservative commentator upon poets and
politics, praised Crabbe in a versified essay entitled *Common
Sense*:

We still have bards, who with aspiring head,
Rise o'er the crazed, the dying, and the dead.
For instance, there's old Crabbe—though some may deem
He shows small taste in choosing of a theme;
None but a bard his own true lines can tell—
He chooses right who executes it well.
And Crabbe has done it well: although his verse

> Be somewhat rude, 'tis pregnant, strong and terse:
> And he has feeling—I who never weep,
> And o'er a Werther's woes am apt to sleep,
> Even I, though somewhat rude, can feel for wo
> Such as I've known, or such as I may know;
> Even I can feel at tales of love or strife,
> Stamped, as are his, with traits of real life,
> He knows the human heart (which, by the way,
> Is more than some Psychologists can say.)
> He knows it well; and draws with faithful pen,
> Not Corsairs, Pedlars, Waggoners,—but Men.
> And then his back-ground—how the figures glow
> With all the mimic art of Gerald Dow,
> Each in itself a picture—while the soul
> Of one great moral breathes thoughout the whole.[20]

A number of Crabbe's conservative qualities are referred to in these densely allusive lines. For instance, his matter-of-factness, which irritated both Wordsworth and Coleridge, is here made matter for admiration and contrasted to those unlikelihoods that for a Neoclassicist make Goethe's *Werther* sentimental, or to those psychological "systems" that make Byron's corsair and Wordsworth's waggoner unrealistic. The brushwork of the new mystics seemed, to many, hopelessly blurred next to the sharp sketches of a writer who deserved comparison with the seventeenth-century Dutch realist Dow, whom Crabbe in the first of the *Posthumous Tales* calls "a famed master." "Hogarth of song!" exclaims a laudatory address to Crabbe by another contemporary.[21]

Notwithstanding Crabbe's faithfulness of description, that "mimic art," Terrot considered him a describer of what is widely representative of persons and events "Such as I've known, or such as I may know . . . ." Then, too, conservative readers like Terrot admired Crabbe for retaining Neoclassical poetic devices. His versification may strike a devotee of Pope as "somewhat rude," but it is "pregnant, strong and terse." The year before Terrot's poem was published, the fluid and unclassical "cockney" heroics of Keats's *Endymion* had appeared and those of Moore's *Lalla Rookh* the year before that. But what above all attracted older readers of Crabbe and eventually alienated young ones was that "one great moral" breathing "throughout the whole."

Not that the Romantics turned their backs upon morality. Quite the contrary—Wordsworth and Shelley, for example, were passionately convinced that they were profound moralists. But the Romantic morality was untraditional, still experimental, organic. Crabbe continued to support the established, long-familiar code whose roots lay ultimately in the medieval scorn of the world.

Having lost much of its religious basis in the willful rationalism of the late Renaissance, this older "system" had reestablished itself on secular grounds: not now apprehension lest mortal pleasures prevent the realization of immortal joys, rather, the insistence that man's passions lead to pain by disordering his mortal life. Earth having replaced heaven as man's certain abode, reason had had to replace faith as man's true mode. Values eternal because divinely ordained and sanctioned had ceded to values eternal because demonstrably efficient and universal. But this "mighty static metaphysic" was finally beginning to crumble altogether,[22] and the admonishments of Crabbe's verse met ready acquiescence among readers who felt the need of buttresses against the time's rising tides—new ranges of emotion, new visions, reassociations of the sensibilities. To those who could not see that the new poets were as legitimately convinced that reason lay with them as the older ones had been, Crabbe was a solid rock, one of the few left to "Rise o'er the crazed, the dying and the dead."

Trusting instinct above precept, the unconscious above the conscious, was of course no newer idea in Western history than was trusting pure reason. It was not even suddenly reintroduced by the Romantics. The "reasonable" century itself had throughout been fascinated by the question of "natural" feelings, their source and relative trustworthiness. Swift's appealing (but comic) quadrupeds, the Houyhnhnms, are at least as respondent to instinct as his repulsive bipeds, the Yahoos. And, like Swift, to whom, in fact, Crabbe bears some unexpected resemblances, Crabbe belongs among those who could not trust that *natural* and *divine* were any more surely synonymous than *ratiocination* and *God's will*. Fancy, dangerous imp, can be bred in either head or heart. The pessimism of Swift and Crabbe is tinged with a disillusionment one is tempted to call post-Romantic. Crabbe's reminiscence of himself as a boy in *Tales of the Hall,* that passage beginning, " 'I loved to walk where none had walk'd before,' " is soon followed by its own rebuke become explicit:

> "Thus, with my favorite views, for many an hour
> Have I indulged the dreams of princely power;
> When the mind, wearied by excursions bold,
> The fancy jaded, and the bosom cold,
> Or when those wants that will on kings intrude,
> Or evening-fears, broke in on solitude;
> When I no more my fancy could employ,
> I left in haste what I could not enjoy,
> And was my gentle mother's welcome boy."

The limitations of romantic experience are expressed with peculiar and eminently Crabbean poignance in the concluding sentence, which simultaneously questions the romantic impulse, as does so much of Crabbe's work, and betrays still a subterranean sympathy for that impulse. At least as early as 1780, Crabbe had announced his intention to commit himself wholly to neither heart nor head, and to become, as poet, neither "crazed" by exaltation, to use Terrot's word, nor dehumanized by the prosaic. "Receive," he had asked in *The Candidate,* "a bard, who neither mad nor mean,/Despises each extreme, and sails between . . . ."

Crabbe's value as an interpreter of life does not lie in the exposition of a rapidly dating rationalistic system, even though numerous of his contemporaries assumed so. And he wasn't interested in buttressing such a system with theological niceties themselves as dated. The spiritual and intellectual dignity of his poetry comes from something more, too, than his responsible period painting, his thorough social documentation, or his meticulously horizontal vision (for thus does E. M. Forster describe Crabbe's refusal as poet to see the divine in sky, sea, or marsh[23]). It comes from the fact that Crabbe had, after all, a comprehensive "vision of the world as a whole"; there is, in fact, "nothing in Crabbe of exact portraiture"—after looking about the world with care, he "thought out his visions till they came back to him in another form."[24] Beneath the factual surface of his verse lies a pattern of human experience which could qualify him for, at the least, what Morse Peckham has called "negative romanticism" and perhaps for "positive romanticism." More significantly, it allies him to figures remote in time, place, and culture—to Aeschylus or T.S. Eliot, to Dante or Dostoevski.

The pattern, not fully realized in *The Borough* because not yet fully realized in Crabbe's own experience, can be abstractly expressed in Peckham's words describing the growth of a Romantic's mind: "A man moves from a trust in the universe to a period of doubt and despair of any meaning in the universe, and then to a re-affirmation of faith in cosmic meaning and goodness, or at least meaning."[25] In Crabbe's mature poetry this pattern is played out in terms of crime, or sin, punishment, atonement, and redemption. These are the central terms of the religion Crabbe professed, but they are not peculiar to Christianity nor does Crabbe insist on calling its stages peculiarly Christian conditions. Whatever modern reader is offended by the pervasive air of the didactic in Crabbe ought to remember that Crabbe is one of the least didactic of English clergyman-poets. Nevertheless, whoever shrinks from Crabbe's touch while pitying him his old-fashioned moral severity, is more than likely to be suffering an unacknowledged twinge of guilt. Crabbe's morality is practical, terrestrial, and yet universal. He suspects, with a twentieth-century Romantic, that

each man is not only himself, he is also the unique, quite special, and in every case the important and remarkable point where the world's phenomena converge, in a certain manner, never again to be repeated. For that reason the history of everyone is important, eternal, divine. For that reason every man, so long as he lives at all and carries out the will of nature, is wonderful and worthy of every attention. In everyone has the spirit taken shape, in everyone creation suffers, in everyone is a redeemer crucified.[26]

Crabbe's reliance on the "reasonable" approach to life actually leads him to an essentially imaginative perception. Reason dissuades him from indulging in those speculative, vertical approaches to the divine; but it does not object to his escaping horizontal confinement by means of metaphor. In the words of a Victorian Romantic, "Looking straight out is," after all, "looking straight down";[27] and, in the words of a Victorian

Modern, "the punishments which religious fables threaten the dead with are, for the most part, symbols for the actual degradation which evil-doing brings upon the living; so that the fear of hell is not more deterrent or repressive than experience of life would be if it were clearly brought before the mind."[28] Crabbe's determination to bring before his readers' minds the hellishness of much terrestrial experience—in "Peter Grimes," for instance—is matched by a morbid preoccupation with the subterranean life of the guilt stricken and with the sufferings of social and moral isolation. He moves well beyond this Byronic obsession, however, in *Tales of the Hall*, where the redemptory process comes to figure as importantly as the damnatory. But this full vision, encompassing its faint but "Everlasting Yea" as well as its sonorous "No," is only beginning to emerge in the set of unrelated tales he published in 1812.

II *Twenty-one Tales in Verse*

The 1812 *Tales in Verse* is the most difficult of Crabbe's works to characterize or to describe. Because his critics had considered the sketches of *The Register* superficially linked and the scheme of *The Borough* distracting, Crabbe did not try to make the parts of his two new volumes parts of a whole. Neither Boccaccio nor Chaucer, he points out in his Preface, was fully successful in adopting an "artificial mode of affinity," so why, he asks, should I make such an attempt? Freed thereby from an inherited and somewhat hampering literary habit, Crabbe presents his twenty-one new pieces not as portions of a long survey poem but simply as what they are: unrelated narratives as often unlike as similar. The only way to appreciate "the generous range and sweep" of Crabbe's art in this new publication, as Whitehead reminds us, is to read the work itself. Only then can the reader discover "the remarkable variety of emotions, themes and artistic purposes to which the Tale lends itself in Crabbe's hands."[29]

Some of these twenty-one tales are comic, some pathetic, some tragic. Some are fully plotted, some prefer situation to incident, and some are character sketches developed through events presented chronologically. Some are conventional in subject matter, others experimental; some are in purpose didactic, and others reserve judgment.

Among the amusing ones, like "The Dumb Orators" (I), "The Lover's Journey" (X), and "The Wager" (XVIII), the most consistently humorous is "The Frank Courtship" (VI); but even it contains some of that high seriousness which marks all of Crabbe's work. For comedy of manners, this firmly textured poem surpasses *The Borough*'s "Vicar" in originality, range, and depth. It is Crabbe's wittiest and warmest variation on a favorite subject—the influence which intercourse with a relative or friend may have upon a character not yet wholly formed. The widowed aunt whom Sybil Kindred lives with for some years is just the sort—whist-loving and worldly—who in another tale might contaminate an impressionable niece. Instead, the aunt's influence is wholesome. Sybil's suitor, grave and sober as he is, would not have fallen in love with her at their first meeting had she remained untouched by the years spent in that gayer, more spontaneous household. For Sybil had been reared in an atmosphere of Cromwellian austerity. The inflexibility of her father's character is established for us in the poem's opening lines:

> Grave Jonas Kindred, Sybil Kindred's sire,
> Was six feet high, and look'd six inches higher;
> Erect, morose, determined, solemn, slow,
> Who knew the man, could never cease to know;
> His faithful spouse, when Jonas was not by,
> Had a firm presence and a steady eye;
> But with her husband dropp'd her look and tone,
> And Jonas ruled unquestion'd and alone.

Crabbe has already introduced several of the ambivalences that crowd this tale and are its strength and subtlety. The words "faithful" and "alone," for example, are not flatly used; they raise suggestions as to the couple's relationship that are relevant to matter later in the story. Five hundred lines later, Sybil herself has defied her formidable father and rebuked the suitor he has chosen for her.

But she has not rejected that suitor. She has judged him according to what she thinks are her own lights. Actually, she has honored her father's wishes after all; and, although she owes her becoming temerity to the aunt, she has inherited her level-headedness from the father. Rebellious yet not disobedient, independent but malleable, her father's daughter though her aunt's protegée, bold but feminine, Sybil is conceived in depth. Crabbe celebrates through her the nuptials of sense and sensibility. The apparently tyrannical father turns out to have his third dimension too, as does the grave suitor who commences his addresses calm and confident and concludes them troubled and uncertain.

The courting scene, with Sybil and Josiah redefining such concepts as compliment and reproof, is social comedy of superior kind. Ironies give dimension to what could have remained simply an amusing situation. From this scene the tale gets its name, but less than a quarter of the poem is devoted to it. That is why the scene is so very successful. Crabbe has prepared for it by giving us a hundred lines of parental maneuverings preliminary to the prearranged courtship. Before these, another one hundred fifty lines have established with exactness the sober, well-regulated life and opinions of the dissenting Kindred clan, the particular traits of Sybil, her parents, and her aunt, and the recently altered tenor of Sybil's life. Futhermore, the poem continues some forty-five lines after the courting scene has ended, and wit and suspense are maintained until the final word. Convinced that in this, their first interview, his "thoughtless" and "stubborn" daughter has hopelessly insulted her proud suitor, Jonas interrogates Sybil while the perturbed Josiah wanders in the garden. Jonas will not hide his anger or, we see, his still unextinguished hopes:

> "Sybil," said he, "I long, and yet I dread
> To know thy conduct—hath Josiah fled,
> And, grieved and fretted by thy scornful air,
> For his lost peace betaken him to prayer?
> Couldst thou his pure and modest mind distress,
> By vile remarks upon his speech, address,
> Attire, and voice?"—"All this I must confess."—
> "Unhappy child! what labour will it cost
> To win him back!"—"I do not think him lost."
> "Courts he then, trifler, insult and disdain?"—
> "No: but from these he courts me to refrain."—

"Then hear me, Sybil: should Josiah leave
Thy father's house?"—"My father's child would grieve."—
"That is of grace; and if he come again
To speak of love?"—"I might from grief refrain."—
"Then wilt thou, daughter, our design embrace?"—
"Can I resist it, if it be of grace?"—
"Dear child! in three plain words thy mind express—
Wilt thou have this good youth?"—"Dear father! yes."

Jeffrey noticed that "The Frank Courtship" contained "even less than Mr. Crabbe's usual moderate allowance of incident."[30] Stories like "Squire Thomas" (XII) or "The Confidant" (XVI) do please us for containing more than Crabbe's usual allowance, but this poem is impressive for the very reason that out of so simple, if not so trite, a situation as a courtship scene Crabbe makes so much and shapes so well what he makes of it.

Well shaped too and richer in incident are "The Parting Hour" (II), "The Brothers" (XX), and "Procrastination" (IV)—all differingly good examples of Crabbe's once widely admired powers of pathos. The first of these looks forward to the farewell-and-return scheme Crabbe adopted for most of the pieces in his *Posthumous Tales,* that of skipping over a large period of time and juxtaposing characters or situations as they now are to what they long ago had been. "Then," he writes:

we at once the work of Time survey,
And in an instant see a life's decay:
Pains mix'd with pity in our bosom rise,
And sorrow takes new sadness from surprise.

A poem of nostalgia, of sorrow, and of sadness, "The Parting Hour" is remarkably free from the too-easy sentiment that weakens Crabbe's last work. Significantly, Crabbe does not award his reunited lovers the serenity in age they might seem to deserve, nor does he exploit to the full the possibilities of poignancy in their long separation.

When, one "autumnal eve," returning Allen disembarks upon his native shore, he sadly contemplates the spot where he stood forty years before to say goodby to Judith. After he becomes reunited with her, the couple mourns together the separate ways each so long followed and when each became married to someone else, he happily and she unhappily. But Crabbe's disarmingly honest focus does not come to rest on these matters. It rests on Allen wandering for weeks through his native village, a lonely ghost amidst ghosts of the past, and on unselfish Judith tenderly caring for him in his final decay, listening patiently as he broods, sometimes in delirium, on memories of other countries, other decades, and other persons— memories not of Judith but of his wife and children, not even of his life with Judith before the long separation but of the years of separation, his "best days."

To compare "The Parting Hour" and "Procrastination" is to be reminded of the allied vignettes in *The Register*, but now each variation covers a much broader canvas. In both tales, a lover goes off to a foreign country to make the fortune he must have to marry his beloved, and in both his return is too long delayed. The marriages do not occur. Both tales achieve pathos through irony, and both are suffused with Crabbe's strong and saddening sense for mutability, for he had an acute awareness of the ways whereby time causes unforeseen and usually un- desired mutations in character and disarrangements of situation. In both tales the man becomes feeble and dependent; in both, one of the lovers becomes contaminated by self-regard. But the self-regard of Allen is nothing compared to Dinah's. In Dinah's heart, *luxuria* replaced love years before Rupert re- turned to marry her. Initiated into the pleasures of money by a wealthy aunt, Dinah had early allowed her affection for the hard-working lover overseas to wane. Having later in- herited the aunt's money, she rejects Rupert utterly when he returns, for he comes to her as poor as when he left. She masks her self-regard under the guise of piety; and, when we last see the couple, Dinah's long-exercised hypocrisy is success- fully resisting final twinges of goodness and conscience. She has come unexpectedly upon Rupert, now a charity case, in a public street:

> Some thoughts of pity raised by his distress,
> Some feeling touch of ancient tenderness;
> Religion, duty, urged the maid to speak

In terms of kindness to a man so weak;
But pride forbad, and to return would prove
She felt the shame of his neglected love;
Nor wrapp'd in silence could she pass, afraid
Each eye should see her, and each heart upbraid.
One way remain'd—the way the Levite took,
Who without mercy could on misery look,
(A way perceived by craft, approved by pride):
She cross'd, and pass'd him on the other side.

Like "The Brothers," in which a returning sailor finds in-
gratitude among those relatives who ought to love him most,
"Procrastination" is actually a much expanded and reconceived
form of a piece from *The Register*. As Arthur Sale has demonstrated, the difference between Crabbe's handling of Catherine
Lloyd, a figure in a "monograph," and Dinah, a character in
a short story, illustrates the advances Crabbe's art has made in
half a decade.[31] Disproportionate amounts of description and
moralizing have given way to deeper probing of character, to
more incident, and to sophisticated dialogue.

"Procrastination" is a more successful poem than several of
the tales in which Crabbe aims at something grander than ironic
pathos. "The Patron" (V), "Edward Shore" (XI), "Resentment" (XVII), and "The Struggles of Conscience" (XIV) have
tragic pretensions. All four are interesting, here and there powerful; but two are marred by flaws of the kind one comes to
fear even in Crabbe's best work. "The Struggles of Conscience"
is a ruthless examination of the skill with which we go through
life salving our protesting consciences until it is too late to
escape the awful retribution which a conscience long denied
must exact. The story's flesh-and-blood characters suffer, though,
from too much association, as it were, with personification. The
main incident, Fulham's intentional ensnarement of his wife
in an adulterous affair, is arresting; but Conscience, "man's
deadliest foe," is the tale's second main character. And her
presence and speeches reduce Fulham's tragedy to a vividly
illustrated sermon.

The other less satisfying of the four tales is "The Patron,"
the kind of tale—there are other examples—in which one suspects Crabbe of stacking cards to pay off old grudges. Crabbe

had for decades received little attention from the noble family
to whom, hopefully, he had kept on dedicating volumes; and,
although in this poem the young literary hopeful deserves
punishment for foolish behavior, the severe punishment he
receives—insanity and an early death—ill fits the crime. We
sense in the poem an unjustified anger towards the somewhat
inconsiderate but far from criminal noble patron.

The insanity which overtakes Edward Shore may be a late
eighteenth-century sort—not quite called for and rather genteel—
but the tale becomes, after its ponderous launching, quite remarkable. More concretely than "The Struggles of Conscience,"
it handles a theme frequent in the Elizabethan dramas Crabbe
admired: "the deforming of a creature in its origin bright and
good, by its own willed persistence in acts against its own
nature."[32] Bright and good indeed, Shore undergoes his regrettable transformation only gradually—until the central incident
occurs, his uneasy seduction of his best friend's wife. The double
betrayal happens when the trusting friend is called out of
town and leaves the couple, already half in love, alone in
his house for some days. Crabbe's handling of the incident
lacks frankness but not impact. He does not dwell upon the
seduction itself. He does not need to. The approaches to it are
sufficient:

> The youth with troubled eye the lady saw,
> Yet felt too brave, too daring to withdraw;
> While she, with tuneless hand the jarring keys
> Touching, was not one moment at her ease.
> Now would she walk, and call her friendly guide,
> Now speak of rain, and cast her cloak aside;
> Seize on a book, unconscious what she read,
> And restless still, to new resources fled;
> Then laugh'd aloud, then tried to look serene,
> And ever changed, and every change was seen.

The last passages of "Edward Shore" describe Shore long after
he has lost his reason but when he has regained tranquillity.
Still in his young manhood, he has fallen into second childhood. His companions now are the children of the neighbor-
hood with whom he plays leapfrog and his onetime sweetheart; upon her pitying face he alertly gazes, straining to

comprehend something, "Like a pleased infant, who has newly caught/From the maternal glance a gleam of thought."

The central incident of "Resentment," a poem based upon "some realities in the history of Mrs. Elmy, the mother of the Poet's wife,"[33] is of a yet more morbid cast. Widowed at forty, a wealthy merchant successfully woos a middle-aged woman who has previously mistrusted ardent wooers and rapturous lovers. He has won his Ellen by being calculatingly cool. Ellen is, as a result, so utterly trusting a wife that later in their married life, when her husband faces bankruptcy, she becomes his easy victim, unwittingly signing away her entire fortune to him. He loses it all, his deception is exposed, and she becomes his implacable foe. Her refusal to forgive him becomes vengeance on a grand scale, and separated from her he dies a pauper. But he dies on the day she has self-righteously decided to send her servant to him with gifts of food and wine as testimony of her charity and to remind him once again of his wickedness. When the servant returns to report in somewhat maudlin terms that he has just died, Ellen realizes too late the enormity of her behavior. Like "The Brothers," in which Isaac too late confesses to himself his own flaw, "Resentment" moves a step further than "Procrastination." The unrelenting, unremorseful Dinah was last seen taking the way the Levite took; Ellen's final words are few as she interrupts her voluble servant: " 'Blame me not, child; I tremble at the news.' " But like Ferdinand's famous one-line utterance upon viewing the Duchess of Malfi dead, Ellen's words point beyond guilt and suffering towards the repentance which the futility of remorse can arouse. Her words, too, have the ring of tragedy.

Some of the *Tales* do not fall readily into such traditional classifications as tragedy, the pathetic, or the comic. "Squire Thomas," for example, is a well-executed, non-tragic tale of busy avarice and unmitigated hatreds played out by characters as forbidding as the blacker schemers of seventeenth-century drama. As unclassifiable and even more harrowing is "The Mother" (VIII). Like D. H. Lawrence's famous "Rockinghorse Winner," it is reminiscent of fairytale and has a post-Freudian tone. Dorothea, a beautiful, vain, and quite loveless woman, who after twelve years of marriage has driven her suffering husband to his grave (he only "then her praise obtained,/ Grav'd on a marble tomb, where he at peace remain'd"), now demands that her younger daughter delay marrying an attentive, quite eligible rector until her elder sister has found a husband. This elder daughter is as beautiful and vain as her mother and as thoroughly spoiled by her as Dorothea once was by *her* parents, who had been bewitched by their child's beauty even as a baby. They had

> watch'd their treasure with peculiar care.
> The fairest features they could early trace,
> And, blind with love, saw merit in her face—
> Saw virtue, wisdom, dignity, and grace. . . .

None of these qualities did their spoiled Dorothea develop. Reared by such a creature, Dorothea's elder daughter could not acquire such qualities either. Her younger one, however, has grown up mild tempered, pious, affectionate—for she is plain.

When the elder sister dies before marrying, the mother insists that Lucy marry not her patient rector but her dead sister's suitor. Lucy refuses; but the rector, unable to avail against the resolute mother, marries someone else. Lucy pines away into religiosity and dies, blissfully convinced at the end that she has become the bride of Christ. The mother lives on untouched by what she has caused, insisting that her own waning beauty remains intact, even as she recounts to parasitic friends, willing to flatter,

> How triumph'd beauty in the days of old;
> How, by her window seated, crowds have cast
> Admiring glances, wondering as they pass'd;
> How from her carriage as she stepp'd to pray,
> Divided ranks would humbly make her way;
> And how each voice in the astonish'd throng
> Pronounced her peerless as she moved along.
> Her picture then the greedy dame displays;
> Touch'd by no shame, she now demands its praise;
> In her tall mirror then she shows a face,
> Still coldly fair with unaffecting grace;
> These she compares: "It has the form," she cries,

But wants the air, the spirit, and the eyes;
This, as a likeness, is correct and true,
But there alone the living grace we view."
This said, th' applauding voice the dame required,
And, gazing, slowly from the glass retired.

Reminding us that it is difficult to generalize about Crabbe's narratives, "The Mother" reminds us too that many such generalizations are especially inept in the light of this 1812 volume. Our limited sampling in the preceding pages shows the ineptness of the most common one: that Crabbe's material is always the same and his subject matter, therefore, drastically limited. A writer who, like Crabbe, adopts a moral viewpoint and impresses it upon his readers by devices sometimes obvious has not necessarily turned his back upon all but one plot and a few stock characters. Crabbe's characters are a varied lot even as types, and some are individualized. His subjects are as various.

So, too, are the poetic devices which his respect for the couplet permits him. One of the inadequate generalizations about his work is that his couplet falls as far beneath Pope's in variety as in sophistication. Truer is it that Crabbe's surpasses Pope's in the particular uses to which it is put. His dialogue in the *Tales* is neither stiff nor singsong—the conclusion of "The Frank Courtship" shows Crabbe's ability to preserve nuances of realistic conversation in the amber of high artifice. With equal ease Crabbe handles narrative, whether rapid (as when he gives synopses of events) or leisurely (as when the forward movement is usefully impeded by dialogue, descriptions, and commentary). And within the limits of what Haddakin has called the "neutral tone" of his verse, Crabbe manages many tonal effects. His "neutrality" is not so much monotonous as low pitched. Next to the orchestrations of Spenser, Shakespeare, Milton, and most of the Romantics, the sounds of Crabbe ring dim; but the ear which adjusts itself to the limitations of the instrument and to its eccentricities discovers its potential.

Another misleading generalization about Crabbe's tales is that they are essentially the same in structure. Naïve in technique, banal in moral, each is assumed to trace the life of a person whose unchanging character is early described for us rather than created in action and dialogue, and whose progress, like that of Hogarth's rake, is always downward—downward until Crabbe, the inveterate divine, can, by editorial interruption or manipulation of dialogue, round everything off with the admonishment that he has been waiting to make from the beginning. We have already seen, however, that some of the *Tales* lead not downward but upward. Others lead neither up nor down but to a changed situation. "The Gentleman Farmer" (III) is one such tale. It is also, in part, a satiric reversal of the decline of a rake. The promiscuous, atheistic, intemperate Gwyn ends up not only properly married but utterly dependent upon a spiritual adviser (the evangelical Wisp) and a doctor of sorts (his wife's cousin); and he is now perfectly happy in his dependencies. The subtle "downward" progress in "Arabella" (IX) can be less simply discounted: the very question with which we are left, whether the rationalizing Arabella ends up a sounder or a less sound human being, is the poem's real point, as Crabbe's apologetic footnote to the tale inversely proves.

"Arabella" and a dozen other tales are examples of the life-history technique Crabbe did too frequently employ—but, as with "Arabella," he could employ it with complete success. In many tales he allots so much space to a particular incident or two that the effect is distinctly different. "The Dumb Orators" is a good example of how far from the chronological biography Crabbe could stray when he was so inclined. So is "The Lover's Journey." The greater part of either tale treats the events of only certain hours during only a few days.

As for that ministerial close with which, it is sometimes claimed, Crabbe's narratives all die away, such conclusions are atypical in *Tales*. Of the twenty-one pieces in the collection, a third do conclude rather patly; but more than a third leave the reader to draw the not necessarily obvious moral himself: "The Dumb Orators," "The Parting Hour," "Procrastination," "The Frank Courtship," "The Mother," "Edward Shore," "Squire Thomas," "The Confidant," and "The Brothers." The moral problem raised in each of the remaining five of the twenty-one is left unresolved and may be unresolvable. What, for example, are we to say of the reformed Farmer Gwyn? He has abandoned his bad ways, yes, and his rash pride has been chastened, but he has been duped by three schemers whose comforts and security his fortune now maintains. Or what of "The Convert" (XIX), to which Crabbe appends a moral requiem that does not resolve the contradictions implicit in John Dighton's reform and fall? Even less do "Arabella," "The Squire and the Priest" (XV), and "Resentment" lend themselves to easy readings. By 1812 Crabbe was no closer than in 1807 to being the smug clergyman his times easily produced.

What best distinguishes *Tales in Verse* from *The Borough*, and in so doing identifies it as a midway point between *The Borough* and *Tales of the Hall*, is the number of narratives in which unhappiness or suffering is either avoided or overcome. Tales with happy endings do not, however, make up the majority of this volume's pieces; for the word "happy" can be applied to events, persons, or situations in Crabbe's poetry only with special caution. Jubilation is never his concluding note. Even in "The Frank Courtship," in which the lovers are surely headed for a successful marriage, we misread if we assume that the course of their relationship will run more smoothly after marriage than it already has. One of Crabbe's theses, allying him to the post-Romantic novelists he influenced, is that obstacles to happiness within marriage are greater and can be more destructive than those which lovers traditionally face before marriage.

The "happy ending" of "The Widow's Tale" (VII) lies in fastidious Nancy's willingness to give up notions of a romantic marriage and settle for an unromantic, ordinary farmer—romantic lovers, her aunt warns from experience, "'plan so wildly, and are wise too late.'" "Arabella" ends "happily" because the once very proper Arabella is now willing, since she has begun to age, to settle for a not-so-very proper husband. Jesse of "Jesse and Colin" (XIII) guarantees herself a degree of happiness by accepting honest Colin and his poverty in place of a wealthy relative and her household of clever sycophants. Farmer Jones's free-thinking son, in "The Learned Boy" (XXI), is guaranteed his happier future by a horse whipping which knocks his too freely wandering thoughts back into proper place again.

But only in the happy solution to "The Confidant," the volume's most skillfully handled tale (Charles Lamb turned it into a toned-down play), does the concluding satisfaction we feel derive more from our response to warmth of feeling than from our admission that cool-headed compromise is wise. This tale's warmth comes from our discovery that Stafford, the husband, besides despising the villainess of the piece, his wife's false friend, and arranging her humiliating exposure, also lovingly forgives his wife the premarital affair (and its illegitimate offspring) which has made her the victim of blackmail. Ellen Orford's submissiveness in the face of multiple disasters was an acceptance fruitful however incredible, and it anticipated tales Crabbe was yet to write. Now "The Confidant" anticipates the controlling temper of *Tales of the Hall*. In some of the *Tales in Verse*—"The Brothers," "Jesse and Colin," "Resentment," even "Arabella"—Crabbe explores aspects of forgiveness or reconciliation, themes so important to his next volume. Only in "The Confidant," however, does the experiential pattern incomplete in *The Borough* find true completion: guilt, suffering, and remorse lead at last to a climax of affirmation.

The release into affirmation comes late in Crabbe's career but not unreasonably so. There is no other route to this kind of affirmation than through negation, in whose shadowed valley Crabbe long had been. The introductory link of the twelfth tale of Crabbe's novel in verse, *Tales of the Hall*, contains a morbid but striking conceit (Blake used it too). When a rector is asked why he has delayed so long in making a visit, his questioner offers as possible reasons the christening of a dying baby:

> "Or wert thou call'd, as parish priest, to give
> Name to a new-born thing that would not live,
> That its weak glance upon the world had thrown,
> And shrank in terror from the prospect shown. . . ."

Elsewhere in the work the speaker's brother uses the equally striking phrase "the grand disease of life." To Crabbe the world does present a terrible prospect, and the living of life is like succumbing to a disease. But the way down becomes the way up. Crabbe is not a nihilist or even a pessimist. A new-born thing may easily be conceived as shrinking back terror-struck towards the comforts of oblivion, but it is the real duty of man to move forward—to move upward because he has had the courage to see downward. The only optimism worth its name is that which begins with the premise that there is terror to be faced, adversity to be overcome, and disaster merely to be accepted—including the first of all disasters, being born. Man's condition as a victim of the grand disease of life has taken on in Crabbe's poetry before 1819 proportions pathetic or tragic. In *Tales of the Hall,* the proportions expand to the nearly heroic.

III *Our Tale of Tales*

"I think," John Masefield has said of Crabbe, "that he had vision of those powers which watch and punish, in strange ways, even after long delay . . . . according to his power, he was not far from the heart of life."[34] We have seen how shadows of the punishing powers fall long and dark across *The Borough.* And we have recognized that the acrid taste of *The Village,* that more confused treatise on outrages committed by man and nature, is that of universal guilt. The village's poorhouse, whose description so affected young Wordsworth, was really the world in miniature, one in which the sanity we all expect to retain seems only to guarantee the misery we all hope to escape:

> There children dwell, who know no parents' care;
> Parents, who know no children's love, dwell there!
> Heart-broken matrons on their joyless bed,
> Forsaken wives, and mothers never wed;
> Dejected widows with unheeded tears,
> And crippled age with more than childhood fears;
> The lame, the blind, and, far the happiest they!
> The moping idiot and the madman gay.

Personal memories troublesomely recent when Crabbe composed *The Village* darken its vision of life unreasonably. When, a quarter of a century later, he was conceiving *The Borough's* microcosmic prisons within the grand macrocosmic one, Crabbe was still unable to recollect in sufficient tranquillity those early years in that bleak village by the sea and the "bold,

artful, surly, savage race" that inhabited it. Life in the mean-
time had not offered enough in the way of mitigation. Both
poems contain an autobiographical excess which the universal
truths embodied in them cannot fully absorb. It was in part
this pungent residue that offended Hazlitt and led him justly
to remark, in his generally unjust essay, that superior work lay
in the 1812 *Tales*.

Every poem in *Tales* reflects identifiable events or acquaintances out of Crabbe's life, but now such raw material only
rarely overmasters its reshaper or obtrudes upon the reader.
One of the things Crabbe has begun to realize is that the im-
poverished soul is not best represented by an empty purse—or
even by that striking and convincing symbol, a desolate setting.
This realization had caused that confused but prophetic counter-
movement in "Ellen Orford," in which poverty plays as symbol
a triple role. In the first half of the poem, as throughout *The
Village*, poverty represents, rather muddily, both the trans-
gressing soul and the punishment which transgression deserves.
Later, however, it comes to suggest the inexplicably severe
assaults life makes upon man, the grand disease called living.
Ellen's repentant soul proves itself healthy enough to with-
stand all the calamities, even the final one: that of being reduced to absolute poverty. At the tag end of a miserable life,
she looks cheerfully towards her death and announces, "I love
mankind and call my *GOD* my friend." Her final composure
strikes us as forced, her love of man and God as virtually
masochistic. Crabbe has improperly balanced the ingredients
of his tale, possibly because his real but repressed verdict on
life's handling of Ellen was savagely opposed to the poem's
declared one.

At any rate, he clearly does intend to show that moral health
is not the property of the upper classes or of the well-to-do,
any more than happiness is the destiny of all lovers. Ellen is
strongest when she has reached absolute bottom. Crabbe's later
poetry makes even clearer the view that conditions of wealth
and poverty or the stratifications of society, however useful
as symbols, are the accidents of life. Life's real incidents are
the loss of Eden, the accession of woe, the choice of hell or of
trial by purgation—a trial which promises the reconstruction of a

humbler Eden upon the deserted site, an Eden pallid and of the earth earthy but attainable.

Almost the longest of the pieces in *Tales of the Hall* is "Sir Owen Dale," an interesting fusion of early and late Crabbe. One of the few poems by Crabbe that ever displeased his most devoted reader, Edward Fitzgerald, it contains an inner tale that seems out of place in so late a work; it reads as if it had simply been transported here from *The Borough,* for it combines a headlong plunge into poverty with the special vocabulary of damnation. The outer framing tale is of a different tone; in it, harshness accepts rebuke and condemnations melt into forgiveness.

The egotistical widowed Sir Owen has been coquettishly led on to propose to a sprightly young lady, Camilla, who has had no intention of marrying the man and so rejects him with glee. Dedicating his unrequited energies to long-term revenge, the deeply wounded Sir Owen waits until his nephew comes of age and then persuades him to promise to delude Camilla exactly as she deluded him, by courting her in order to jilt her. Part way through the masquerade, however, Charles falls in love with Camilla and she with him; and of course proud Sir Owen, though he listens to their honest confession and understands the situation, cannot now forgive either of them. He binds Charles to his promise not to marry Camilla, then visits a tenant, Ellis, whose wife had years before run away with a lover. The inner tale commences here, for Sir Owen had once seen Ellis inflamed with vengeance, and he wants his own deplorable passion to be flattered and justified by a sympathizer. He listens greedily to Ellis' tale of how the couple's elopement terminated in dreadful poverty.

> "Know you they suffer, Ellis?"—Ellis knew;
> " 'Tis well! 'tis just! but have they all their due?
> Have they in mind and body, head and heart,
> Sustain'd the pangs of their accursed part!"—
> "They have!"—" 'Tis well."—"and wants enough to shake
> The firmest mind, the stoutest heart to break."

The wrongdoers have not escaped the physical punishment which it pleases Sir Owen to know is their due. Crabbe now

interrupts his rapid narration and gives Ellis nearly a hundred
lines for describing the wretched state in which he found
the couple. The description has a peculiar, repulsive power:

> "The roof, unceil'd in patches, gave the snow
> Entrance within, and there were heaps below;
> I pass'd a narrow region dark and cold,
> The strait of stairs to that infectious hold;
> And when I enter'd, misery met my view
> In every shape she wears, in every hue,
> And the bleak icy blast across the dungeon flew;
> There frown'd the ruin'd walls that once were white;
> There gleam'd the panes that once admitted light;
> There lay unsavoury scraps of wretched food;
> And there a measure, void of fuel, stood.
> But who shall part by part describe the state
> Of these, thus followed by relentless fate?
> All, too, in winter, when the icy air
> Breathed its black venom on the guilty pair?"

The realist's description has risen above the literal into the
symbolic. That narrow strait to an infectious hold, the coldness,
the misery—all suggest an icy inferno. The bleak blowing wind
is a detail Crabbe used figuratively in other contexts. In "The
Natural Death of Love" (*Tales of the Hall*, XIV), a "wintry
blast/Moans o'er the place of love and pleasure past"; in "The
Equal Marriage" (*Posthumous Tales*, III), freezing snows and
"angry," frowning clouds oppress the suddenly bankrupt lovers,
who find that their love was too heavily based upon passion.
In both poems and in "Sir Owen Dale" such weathers suggest
both the fact of transgression and the spiritual dungeon to
which the guilty couples are confined. The sense of the inanimate
passing spiritual judgment and exercising punishment is present in "Sir Owen Dale": the assaulting snow, the black air,
and the wind take on in full context strength beyond that of
poetic conceit. Ellis continues his description of this "guilty
pair" pursued by "relentless fate":

> "And in this state—that wife I cannot name
> Brought forth a famish'd child of suffering and shame.
>   "This had you known, and traced them to this scene.

Where all was desolate, defiled, unclean,
A fireless room, and, where a fire had place,
The blast loud howling down the empty space—
You must have felt a part of the distress.

....

The sight was loathsome, and the smell was faint;
And there that wife, whom I had loved so well,
And thought so happy, was condemned to dwell. . . .
There she reclined unmoved, her bosom bare
To her companion's unimpassioned stare,
And my wild wonder—Seat of virtue! chaste,
As lovely once! O! how wert thou disgraced!
Upon that breast, by sordid rags defiled,
Lay the wan features of a famish'd child;—
That sin-born babe in utter misery laid,
Too feebly wretched even to cry for aid. . . ."

The child born of the adulterous union represents the fruits of sin, this wan famished creature. The man is no longer affected by the sight of his mistress' breast. The fire of love is out, the couple left shivering in abject poverty; and where that fire was is now only an emptiness through which blow the winds of despair.

The catalog or repetition of words like "defiled," "unclean," "loathesome," "sordid," "odious," "mean," "foul," and "unwholesome" is more than the depiction of the couple's poverty warrants. Ellis is struck with "wild wonder" at this physical suffering and punishment because the guilty lovers have become something other than human beings. They are medieval personifications of Mankind facing the Reckoning. Ellis tells of his own reaction to this dreadful vision of the eternal mortal trio—the prostrate woman and at "her wither'd breast/The wither'd child" and the man crumpled in guilty self-abasement at their feet:

"Ghastly he smiled;—I knew not what I felt,
But my heart melted—hearts of flint would melt,
To see their anguish, penury, and shame,
How base, how low, how groveling they became.
I could not speak my purpose, but my eyes
And my expression bade the creature rise."

The result of Ellis' vigorous description and his exemplary forgiveness is the melting of Sir Owen's own heart. "Vengeance," exclaims his tenant, "is not ours!" Vengeance has already been wreaked. The symbolic picture and its moral now work so powerfully upon Sir Owen that his excessive pride is broken. Thus chastized, he forgives Charles and Camilla. Whoever discovers with what terrible efficacy the mysterious powers punish, whether at once or after long delay, knows that mercy, forgiveness, and reconciliation are the surpassing mortal virtues—and that they are founded on humility.

The moral of "Sir Owen Dale" is well representative of *Tales of the Hall*. Its technique is not. More representative technically are portions of the seventh part, "The Elder Brother." In it Crabbe's description of a shabby room assails our senses in the way usual with descriptions by this poet of the painstakingly reproduced particular, but it does so in order to define the moral shabbiness of the room's owner. It is not poverty and meanness that have impressed us but disorder and tastelessness, and these are moral qualities.

Crabbe is more convincing yet when he relies even less upon the melodrama of externals for presenting internal states. The greater sufferers in "The Sisters" (*Tales of the Hall*, VII) are not meant to be Lucy and Jane, both of whom imprudently trusted men unworthy of them, but the men whose betrayals have left the sisters so unhappy. Before Jane's essential goodness wins for her the comparative relief of insanity, she claims that her financial losses have made her unbearably poor since they lost her a wooer as well. Lucy replies that the crass, rejecting lover is the worse off: "O! poorer still;/Poorer, my Jane, and far below thee now:/The injurer he,—the injured sufferer thou." Victims are richer of spirit than the victimizers; and, when the sisters reappear in the last book of *Tales of the Hall*, we learn that their presently debilitating griefs could finally beget in them such spiritual force as would, at last, "with gather'd might,/The scatter'd forces of the soul unite." As we shall see, such has been the experience of George, friend to the sisters and the narrator of their history.

Unfortunately, "The Sisters" gives no proof that Lucy's conviction is sound, and we suspect that Crabbe knows it may not be. But other tales do offer proof. We remember that "Resentment" did, for it ended with the injurer beginning to suffer more profoundly than the injured sufferer, now mercifully dead. One of the best pieces in *Tales of the Hall* is "Delay Has Danger," which handles without the obscuring paraphernalia of poverty or physical disintegration a man's gradual descent into hell and his long residence there. Alternating description, dialogue, and comment as ways of conveying his characters' states of being, Crabbe appeals abstractly to our judgment as much as he does concretely to our senses.

The poem's protagonist is Henry, an unexceptional, decent fellow whose pride is pleasantly flattered by the sincere affection of Fanny, the simple but good hearted, "mild and blue-eyed lass" whom he meets on an extended visit away from home. Instead of telling her at the outset that he has a fiancée waiting trustingly for his return, he so encourages Fanny's attentions that soon he could only with difficulty retreat from marrying her. Just before retreat is forever impossible, his eyes are opened by a chill and justly accusing letter from the waiting Cecilia. But his self-regard and his pride, that "high disdain," prevent his turning back. As he reads the letter, he stands virtually at the gate of hell—as if Dante's awful inscription, or Milton's darkness, were already visible to his eyes:

> Henry was lost—his brain confused, his soul
> Dismay'd and sunk, his thoughts beyond control;
> Borne on by terror, he foreboding read
> Cecilia's letter! and his courage fled;
> All was a gloomy, dark, and dreadful view,
> He felt him guilty, but indignant too:—
> And as he read, he felt the high disdain
> Of injured men. . . .

In anger, he blurts out the self-destroying proposal that Fanny has been hoping for and that her guardians have been leading him towards:

> In that weak moment, when disdain and pride,
> And fear and fondness, drew the man aside,
> In this weak moment—"Wilt thou," he began,

"Be mine?" and joy o'er all her features ran;
"I will!" she softly whisper'd; but the roar
Of cannon would not strike his spirit more;
Ev'n as his lips the lawless contract seal'd
He felt that conscience lost her seven-fold shield,
And honour fled; but still he spoke of love,
And all was joy in the consenting dove.
    That evening all in fond discourse was spent,
When the sad lover to his chamber went,
To think on what had past, to grieve and to repent.
Early he rose, and look'd with many a sigh
On the red light that fill'd the eastern sky;
Oft had he stood before, alert and gay,
To hail the glories of the new-born day;
But now dejected, languid, listless, low,
He saw the wind upon the water blow,
And the cold stream curl'd onward as the gale
From the pine-hill blew harshly down the dale.
On the right side the youth a wood survey'd,
With all its dark intensity of shade;
Where the rough wind alone was heard to move,
In this, the pause of nature and of love,
When now the young are rear'd, and when the old,
Lost to the tie, grow negligent and cold—
Far to the left he saw the huts of men,
Half hid in mist, that hung upon the fen;
Before him swallows, gathering for the sea,
Took their short flights, and twitter'd on the lea;
And near the bean-sheaf stood, the harvest done,
And slowly blacken'd in the sickly sun;
All these were sad in nature, or they took
Sadness from him, the likeness of his look,
And of his mind—he ponder'd for a while,
Then met his Fanny with a borrow'd smile.

With his marriage to Fanny, the gates of Inferno close behind him—a lower middle-class inferno, not a poorhouse or a
hovel. He has married one whom he does not love and who
therefore soon loses her love for him. The two come to despise
each other, but "Such was his fate, and he must yet endure/The
self-contempt that no self-love can cure." After enduring such
torment for years, Henry happens to enter a house on business

and comes face to face with Cecilia. The meeting is presented as
if it were a scene of judgment, and so it is:

> Unhappy man! he could not, dared not speak,
> But look'd around, as if retreat to seek;
> This she allow'd not; but, with brow severe,
> Ask'd him his business, sternly bent to hear.
> He had no courage, but he view'd the face
> As if he sought for sympathy and grace;
> As if some kind returning thought to trace—
> In vain; not long he waited, but with air
> That of all grace compell'd him to despair,
> She rang the bell, and, when a servant came,
> Left the repentant traitor to his shame.

The sinner, quailing before the sudden apparition of his judge
but forced to stand fast, turns pitifully and imploringly in an
appeal for grace—that twice-used rhyme word. No grace is
granted. His soul has long ago been weighed and found wanting; hell is where he has been, is, and, at least until death, will
remain.

In the depths of poverty Ellen Orford enjoyed full salvation.
Lapped in physical comforts, characters like Henry or Susan
(*Tales*, XVII) suffer punishment—and selfish, wealthy James of
"The Cousins" (*Posthumous Tales*, XXI) "Feels a keen pang, as
he beholds the door/Where peace abides, and mutters—'I am
poor!'" In a middle-class setting Anna of "The Confidant" was
tormented by one of the long-waiting, watchful, punishing
powers, whose medium was the false friend, Eliza. But also at
work in this setting were the regenerative powers. Anna well
deserved her husband's forgiveness. She had earned a graduation
from purgatory. When the husband expelled Eliza, who is now
the identified injurer and so the greater sufferer, "with troubled
joy the wife/Felt the new era of her changeful life." The
infernal overtones of such tales as "Delay Has Danger" and "Sir
Owen Dale" are frequent in *Tales of the Hall*, but they do
not dominate it as they do *The Borough*. In the 1812 *Tales*
the focus is beginning to shift from earth as prison or hell; in
Tales of the Hall it has turned to the possibilities of escape, of
release during life.

Uncommitted as to the justice of, even as to the existence of heaven, Crabbe the poet discourages blind trust in rewards to be earned either on earth or in an afterlife. Such confidence is as dangerously self-centered as despair, which is blindly confident that there is nothing to place one's trust in anywhere. He preferred not to speculate upon an afterlife: "When thoughts of the fate of those near to me enter my Mind, I confess I banish them as quickly as I can, leaving this mysterious Subject as unrevealed and inexplicable. God is good I say and think no more, that is I dare not think."[35] Life on earth adequately reveals man's nature, nor is the progress of the soul here below wholly inexplicable. The intemperate, the rash, and the arrogant are more likely than not to involve themselves in states of unrest severer than purgative; the temperate, the prudent, and the humble can achieve a serenity beyond purgatory.

The frame device for Crabbe's most optimistic major work, *The Tales of the Hall,* is at last a *natural* "mode of affinity." It permits him to incorporate a quantity of tragic and pathetic narratives, such as he was fond of writing, within an affirmative scheme to which they contribute essential meaning. "Books" I-IV, VI-VII, and XXII (the last) are devoted wholly to this verse-novel's frame and its two main characters. The rest of the "books" are separate tales; but, like those told by Chaucer's pilgrims, each is linked to the frame by introductory descriptions or conversations. Nearly as varied a collection as the 1812 *Tales,* these include such distinct types as tragedies ("Ruth," "Delay Has Danger," "Smugglers and Poachers") and comedies either satiric ("The Preceptor Husband") or happy in conclusion ("William Bailey"), and also two ghost stories.

These ghost stories deserve a moment's notice, for they are a kind of narrative that Crabbe had always classified among the fictions which mislead young or immature minds. For several years he had been planning a series of tales of the supernatural and gathering appropriate plots to versify.[36] What may be unfinished or unrevised versions of two such appear in Pollard's *New Poems by George Crabbe* ("The Insanity of Ambitious Love" and "Where Am I Now?"), and at least two others remain in manuscript ("The Doctor's Ghost" and "Misery"). Most writers and readers can enjoy ghosts for their own sakes. Crabbe apparently could not, as even the more hair-raising of the two pieces in *Tales of the Hall* shows. By title a ghost story, "Lady Barbara; or, the Ghost" is really a study in Oedipal and Electral frustrations, for Crabbe's tales about ghosts must always be studies of the psychology of those who believe that they have seen the ghosts. He allows himself the obvious pleasure of becoming seriously engaged by apparitions, visions, and hauntings only by planning from the outset to define them as sad evidences of intellectual or emotional irresponsibility. Yet they do bear overtones of a non-material reality. Lady Barbara's life is neither more nor less involved in the supernatural than, say, the life of Peter Grimes. Both figures undergo strange spiritual experiences. The deathbed confession of Lady Barbara, sexual transgressor, concludes with terms as baldly archetypal as moral:

> Like the first being of my sex I fell,
> Tempted, and with the tempter doom'd to dwell—
> He was the master-fiend, and where he reign'd was hell.

What is significant about *Tales of the Hall* is not, however, the variety of its tales but the homogeneity of the whole work. Although every tale Crabbe ever wrote glances somewhere at problems of love or marriage, each of the fifteen in *Tales of the Hall* is quite preoccupied with the subject, and so is the frame which contains them. "It is rather remarkable," Jeffrey went as far as to notice, "that Mr. Crabbe seems to become more amatory as he grows older; the interest of almost all the stories in this collection turning on the tender passion, and many of them on its most romantic varieties."[37] Crabbe's attitude towards "the tender passion" and some of its less tender potentials is consistent enough to be itself a shaping force in *Tales of the Hall*. Love is so clearly meant to be the work's controlling theme that Crabbe must have conceived of his newest collection as being a comparatively unified whole—even though he told his publisher that, after the seventh book, the rest might appear "in almost any succession we preferred."[38] More important than the word "almost" is the fact that Crabbe submitted the seventh book after the work had gone to press.

With typical diffidence, he told the publisher to include it or
not at his pleasure. The late composition of this book and the
special role it plays in the total scheme indicate, not indifference
but Crabbe's growing interest in turning a collection of tales
into a verse novel.

No accident is it that "Ruth," a tale of illicit love, desertion,
and suicide, is sandwiched between two frame books which
it bears relevantly upon; no accident either that the tenth book,
"The Old Bachelor," stands in the same relation to the frame
plot and one of its two main characters as does this fifth
book, "Ruth," to the frame plot and the *other* main character.
There are further meaningful counterpartings of tales: "The
Preceptor Husband" (IX), for example, is a lighthearted variant
of that also amusing but very serious, thematically crucial book
"The Natural Death of Love" (XIV). In the later tale "William
Bailey" (XIX), Crabbe arranges a happy ending out of essentially the same material that in "Delay Has Danger" led
earlier to an unhappy one. Finally, "Smugglers and Poachers"
(XXI), a vigorous narrative deriving in part from predicaments
borrowed from *Measure for Measure,* might seem an uncon-
sidered choice for a final tale. It is not. Its indebtedness to its
source becomes a valuable allusion since, like Shakespeare's play,
Tales of the Hall emphasizes the values of mercy, forgiveness,
and confession. Treating of two brothers whose difference in
temperament leads at last to their deaths at each other's hands,
"Smugglers and Poachers" is fittingly placed before the work's
last and most heart-warming book, one in which two brothers
of differing temperaments reach a final and unassailable state
of mutual love.

Approximating the novel in form, *Tales of the Hall* approaches
in substance the long autobiographical poem which such Romantics as Byron and Wordsworth were developing. Surprisingly, perhaps, Crabbe's poem is closer to the philosophic
Wordsworth's *Prelude*—not to be published for another thirty
years—than it is to the narrative poet Byron's *Childe Harold.*
Crabbe hardly bothers to disguise the fact that *Tales of the
Hall* traces phases of the growth of his own mind, even though
this poem's maker appears neither as himself (as in *The Prelude*)
nor in the guise of a single fictional character (as in *Childe*

Harold[39]) but as three characters. Crabbe's son noted in 1834 that the rector Jacques is a portrait of Crabbe as churchman. Less obvious and much more significant is the fact that the novel's two central and fraternal figures are also projections of Crabbe; they are secret sharers, as it were, of both his real and his desired experiences.

Richard, the younger brother, has been able to navigate the dangerous seas of life because he has studied well the charts of precept. He is now as wise as George but happier because he has passed unscathed the Scylla and Charybdis of excessive feeling and excessive ratiocination. George, though, a bachelor, has been overwhelmed by both, having suffered a disastrously romantic love, fallen into cynicism and greed, recovered at death's threshold from an unclassified illness, and at last returned to his native village, where he has bought the hall at Binning he so much admired as a boy. Here he will carefully cultivate the rejuvenation he has begun to feel. He has just invited Richard to visit him.

For years the brothers have but seldom met and then been coolly distant. Now they feel at first uneasy with each other, but "Both wish'd for kindness, and it made them kind," and so they win each other's trust:

> At length affection, like a risen tide,
> Stood still, and then seemed slowly to subside;
> Each on the other's looks had power to dwell,
> And brother greeted brother passing well.

This first wave of disruptive emotion checked, the brothers gradually reach the placidity of mind without which the ensuing tales would remain untold. Their reminiscences begin, and some days thereafter the fifteen exemplary tales. When all is concluded, George receives Richard's promise to bring his wife and children to live near Binning in a house which George has secretly (but with the wife's concurrence) purchased for Richard.

Crabbe began work on *Tales of the Hall* in 1815, two years after his wife's long insanity had ended in death. Within days of her going, he had himself fallen so dangerously ill that his life was despaired of. His recovery marked the beginning of a decade of good health such as he had not enjoyed since young manhood. "It always seemed to be his opinion that at that crisis his system had, by a violent effort, thrown off some weight or obstruction which had been for many years previously giving his bodily condition the appearance of a gradual decline."[40] And when on the first of June, 1814, he arrived in Trowbridge, Wiltshire, as the new rector, he was exchanging eastern England, especially Suffolk and its half century of associations, for a western county of wooded hills, lovely river valleys, rich pasture, and prosperous cities. Instead of magnetic gloomy Aldeburgh, he had within easy reach the elegant city of Bath, at that time England's most fashionable provincial city.

But his new rectory was a lonely one, and he may already have been conceiving the full pattern of *Tales of the Hall* when, in 1816, he abandoned hopes of enlivening his life by remarriage. He had been interested in two women half his age and had been courting them, sight unseen, by mail. "I cannot bear to belong to nobody," he had written to one of them in 1815; "my foolish heart at this time and in spite of Reason and Experience, wants Kindness, Sympathy, Affection."[41] Reason won over the sexagenarian's "foolish heart," bringing him in place of a young wife the more appropriate kindness, sympathy, and affection of his own relatives. In December, 1816, he had his son John and his young wife move in to live with him.

It is not surprising to find Crabbe a year earlier referring to his new efforts as "poetical recollections."[42] Although the pattern of the widower Crabbe's life had in numerous ways resembled that of his fictitious bachelor George, it is revealing that Crabbe should have admitted that his "own partiality is with the Relation of the Brother's, Richard's education if I may so call it . . . ."[43] Richard's education made him one who successfully controls all emotions. Thus perfectly bred and trained, Richard is now humbly wise, unaffectedly well mannered, discreetly sensitive. He is, in truth, too exemplary to be Crabbe, however much Richard's seaside childhood, beautifully described in the second half of the fourth book, recalls Crabbe's. For all his "reproving" tone, the poet who conceived Richard was not self-righteous, and he could not have pretended to pose as an ideal model. "No No," he once exclaimed, "I am not exemplary and half my virtue is unavailing Desire."[44] Richard's is, rather, the life Crabbe would like to have lived. Wary in love but wholly happy in marriage, acting ever according to his trust in sense and his mistrust of passion, impressionable but incorruptible, serene, wise through precept instead of through painful experience, Richard is the object of Crabbe's envy—a fantasy figure, whose wife, Matilda, bears the name of one of Crabbe's daughters-in-law. This "Brother-boy," as George calls him, is simultaneously Crabbe's idealization of himself as he once was and the image of himself as he wished he had become. In creating *Tales of the Hall*, Crabbe tried to remake himself by merging someone he never quite was, Richard, with someone he had almost become, George. In most warm terms, George urges Richard to live with him henceforward:

> ". . . to lose thee, Richard, and with thee
> All hope of social joys—it cannot be.
> Nor could I bear to meet thee as a boy
> From school his parents, to obtain a joy,
> That lessens day by day, and one will soon destroy.
> No! I would have thee, Brother, all my own,
> To grow beside me as my trees have grown:
> For ever near me, pleasant in my sight,
> And, in my mind, my pride and my delight. . . .

Crabbe may have succeeded in this strange task of fusing half-idealized fragments of himself. We have all read Byron on the process; so had Crabbe, and very recently.

> 'Tis to create and in creating live
> A being more intense that we endow
> With form our fancy, gaining as we give
> The life we image . . . .

Crabbe knew only too well that precept is seldom likely to be a satisfactory teacher. The tragic conception of life, Yeats' prerequisite for living, comes chiefly through direct experience. "Ah! fly temptation, youth, refrain! refrain!" cried the parish priest

of *The Register.* "I preach for ever; but I preach in vain." As
a minister, Crabbe could never preach that preaching is a vain
pursuit; as a poet, he could in a rare moment admit his doubts;
and they, whether admitted or concealed, are certainly one
source of the chilling profound melancholy that lies at the
bottom of all his work.

The counteractive warmth which spreads gently in all directions through *Tales of the Hall* comes from a variety of related
sources: from George's affection for Richard, from Richard's for
George, from the reconciliatory progress of their relationship, and
from our perception that George will attain eventually the
serenity his brother already enjoys. George has surely earned
such a reward; it is what only a man chastened by turbulent
or disenchanting experience could achieve. "Did I ever tell
you," Crabbe asked one of those female correspondents, "of
a young Lady here, whom I call and who calls herself my
Friend? And she might be, but she is very young and has never
felt Sorrow nor left the Wing of Affection. She is of Course disposed to think, notwithstanding what old Fellows observe, that
the World is a charming place and the Creatures in it good
humoured and generous and kind and happy . . . ."[45] What
Crabbe's young friend lacked—what Crabbe had to be sure
the reader of his letter had acquired—was the special brand of
humility fostered by the tragic vision. This is also what he
wished for the readers of his poetry, especially of *Tales of the
Hall.*

Self-love and self-effacement's adjustment to the nature of
things are antipodal. Into Crabbe's spiritual hells fall those
whose self-love has too long impeded their adaptation to life,
an adaptation which common sense advocates but zeal despises.
Crabbe strips even hope of its wings, for hope is delusion's
perpetuator. George of *Tales of the Hall* wasted his life's best
years fanning a foolishly romantic flame. He emerged from
his delusion only after he had rediscovered his long-lost beloved
and learned that she had become helplessly depraved. Having
watched her die and having recovered from the shock, he now
finally realizes that he gave

> to a strong delusion all his youth,

Led by a vision till alarm'd by truth.
That vision past, and of that truth possest,
His passions wearied and disposed to rest,
George yet had will and power a place to choose,
Where Hope might sleep, and terminate her views.

George's hell, unlike that of his lost Rosabella, turns out to have been purgatory after all. He is among the fortunate ones. He retains the power of choice and can recoup by readjustment. Binning is the right place to have chosen.

Because Richard has from the beginning expected little of either life or love, he has never had to readjust and has a wife who loves him and whom he loves. When she had admitted her love to him before their marriage, he was filled with emotion; but he purposefully dampened his enthusiasm:

> . . . how strange
Was this new feeling, this delicious change;
That sweet delirium, when I gazed in fear,
That all would yet be lost and disappear.
　　Such was the blessing that I sought for pain,
In some degree to be myself again;
And when we met a shepherd old and lame,
Cold and diseased, it seem'd my blood to tame;
And I was thankful for the moral sight,
That soberized the vast and wild delight.

This passage is likely to be distasteful at first reading. Little wonder, perhaps, that Crabbe's poetry has the reputation of not appealing to younger readers or women. Our post-Romantic sensibilities are offended when Richard expresses thankfulness that the image of his beloved became replaced by or (more distasteful yet) superimposed upon that of an old, diseased shepherd. This disfigured pastoral figure is, of course, a multiple symbol, representing the grand disease of life, the potential mutability of all feelings and relationships, and the fate of those who succumb trustingly to romantic illusion. The erring lovers in "Sir Owen Dale" err, at least, against society in committing adultery; the only error Richard was in danger of making was that of being enthusiastic—he had briefly nourished self-love's hope that he might live forever in a "sweet delirium" of happiness, and this is gross danger, indeed. We see that it is greatly to Richard's credit that he checked himself by subduing passion through exercise of reason and by rebuking the warmth of imagination through invocation of chill metaphors. Richard is as far from infernal anguish as any other character in Crabbe's tales.

Richard could not have been allowed even Crabbe's own outburst "Oh! Sally, how I want you!" in the 1780 London journal kept for Sarah Elmy. Sarah and George received, unfortunately, considerably less than they had hoped for. Love is Crabbe's "soul's resistless lord" in his juvenile verse, a "tyrant king" who keeps him singing all day long of "hearts, raptures, flames"; and among those lovers who "in Cupid's mystic circles move," enjoying "Eternal raptures . . . . Which leave no pang behind," are Mira, a sylvan nymph, and her adoring poetical swain. In those years happiness, beauty, love, and truth—all poetry's handmaidens—were siblings. But as the husband of the fourteenth book of *Tales of the Hall* explains to his wife, all happiness is temporary; most love fades rapidly, and truth is harsh:

> Remember you, my love, the fairy tale,
> Where the young pair were spell-bound in the vale?
> When all around them gay or glorious seem'd,
> And of bright views and ceaseless joys they dream'd. . . .
> ....
> All was so light, so lovely, so serene,
> And not a trouble to be heard or seen;
> Till, melting into truth, the vision fled,
> And there came miry roads and thorny ways instead.

From about 1781 on, the god of love Crabbe had worshiped in undistinguished verse appears no more in the likeness of an Apollo but, in verse much more distinguished, as a dark, imponderable, and dangerous deity.

Occasional tender passages in his work from this time on refer to Mira—reminiscences of early love as well as affecting descriptions of delicate women turning insane; but these passages are transient gleams against the dark current of distress. Like Proserpine, Crabbe found love, after all, a dark lord who takes one underground much of the season. In the margin of a letter Sarah wrote him in 1792, Crabbe sometime afterward wrote beside a tenderly elated passage, "Nothing can be more sincere than this, nothing more reasonable and affectionate; and yet happiness was not granted." Even affection, sincerity, and reasonableness can fail to protect us.

Of all the emotions that encourage self-love, romantic love seemed to Crabbe the most representative, common, and compelling. Thus the ultimate subject of *Tales of the Hall*—that modicum of happiness which humility *does* guarantee—receives its most consistent treatment in love material and its fullest expression through the characters of the affectionate brothers. Metaphysical foils, one of the brothers illustrates the path taken by him who allows love to abuse reason: when self-love dragged George's long-idealized woman to a lonely damnation, it nearly dragged George down too, who then

> Felt all my loss of time, the shameful waste
> Of talents perish'd, and of parts disgraced.
> But though my mind was sane, there was a void—
> My understanding seem'd in part destroy'd;
> I thought I was not of my species one,
> But unconnected, injured and undone!

Richard illustrates the path taken by him whose love submits to reason. But love has a third function: besides being able to punish and reward, it can reconstruct. Through the love he once abused, George is at length to achieve peace. But only if his self-love is first destroyed.

When the woman he loved finally died, George sincerely hoped to mend. Sick at heart, "Conscious of youth's great error—nay, the crime/Of manhood now," he "strove to live." Like other characters in Crabbe who face a reckoning, George is quite conscious of his own guilt. He is more fortunate than those for whom it is too late to mend, to "live"; but he is less fortunate than Sir Owen Dale, whose salvation was achieved, like a Dante's, by looking in on a scene of cosmic judgment and rising from the vision cleansed, humbled. George had no guiding friend, like Virgil or Sir Owen's tenant or the kindly matron who instructed Richard with tales like "Ruth." Wanting precept at the crucial moment, he fell and has had to suffer firsthand the painful access of wisdom.

First he tried to forget his "youth's great error" by turning to business. Selfishness, the prime failing, remained: "A love of money . . . . Came creeping on, and settled in my breast," and his acquired wealth is the sign that he is not yet redeemed. He has learned the value of caution but remains learned too in the ways of zeal. The necessary change of character comes when he falls sick, for

> ". . . sickness brought disgust;
> My peace I could not to my profits trust:
> Again some views of brighter kind appear'd,
> My heart was humbled, and my mind was clear'd;
> I felt those helps that souls diseased restore,
> And that cold frenzy, avarice, raged no more.
> From dreams of boundless wealth I then arose;
> This place, the scene of infant bliss, I chose;
> And here I find relief, and here I seek repose."

The seriously sick man, we know, is often able to evaluate life afresh and wholesomely, for he sees it in the light of imminent lifelessness. Like sickness in the novels of D. H. Lawrence, George's comes in answer to a psychic need.

George effected no rebirth when he "strove to live" by becoming a businessman. Thoroughly successful in business, he began to live successfully only when he nearly died. Recovered, he has retreated to the scene of his childhood. He is beginning over at last. His spirit is sponged clean of the years of spiritual disease and torment. A shy, groping love promises to earn the wealth which zealous self-love could not win. As George concludes his autobiographical reminiscences, we realize that, because his past is a poignant reminder, a real life lies ahead:

> . . . my reform
> Has fears like his, who, suffering in a storm,
> Is on a rich but unknown country cast,
> The future fearing, while he feels the past;
> But whose more cheerful mind, with hope inbued,
> Sees through receding clouds the rising good.

Rarely in Crabbe do symbolic clouds and storms recede instead of gather. George, however, is moving out of darkness into light. He will achieve the "happy" life, but he still lacks someone with whom to share such affection as a man of reason can enjoy. It is at this point, when in answer to this need he has summoned his brother to Binning, that *Tales of the Hall* opens. When it closes, the "rising good" promised at the opening has just been assured. But not without a temporary clouding over. Near the end of the set of linked tales, George temporarily withholds his request that Richard and his wife come to live near him. He still fears that such a request would be imposition, and above all he wishes to avoid trespassing upon another's happiness. He fears the trace of self-love in his desire for affection, and the consequent self-denial makes him melancholy. Meanwhile, Richard, who on George's gentle insistences has long extended his visit, notices an unfamiliar, inexplicable coldness in his wife's letters. So he also is melancholy. Unknown to him, his wife has learned of George's secret hope, for she has received a special visit from the rector, that third *persona*. In her letters she has been restraining her pleasure lest she give the secret away.

The brothers' separate melancholies, the cause of which neither can understand in the other, lead to misunderstanding and even to slight antagonism. But, when all is comprehended, all is well; and we see that with this simple device of misunderstanding Crabbe has set going in the concluding portion of *Tales of the Hall* emotional currents that relate directly to three of the work's subjects—affection, reasonableness, and self-denial. In clearing up the misunderstanding, the final twist is given to two others—reconciliation and happiness.

George's mysterious sickness, like Crabbe's own, brought him to the threshold of an equally extraordinary health. "What marks the artist," Lionel Trilling has written, "is his power to shape the material of pain we all have. . . . We are all ill: but even a universal sickness implies an idea of health."[46] In this, Crabbe's last publication during his lifetime, the pain of life shaped by infernal and purgatorial vision in earlier volumes is at last shaped by a benevolent vision, cautious yet curiously exhilarating. The vision tints Crabbe's novel del-

icately, discreetly, and yet so pervasively that John Henry
Newman was moved to call *Tales of the Hall* "a Classic" and
as such, "whether in conception or execution, one of the most
touching in our language."[47]

With the word "conception" Newman suggests that Crabbe
understood what he was about. *Tales of the Hall* testifies to
Crabbe's own ability to emerge from darkness into light; it
testifies to his discovery, if not of *solution* at least of *defense*.
It is also a declaration of his will to believe in mankind's
ability to discover the same. Crabbe stubbornly hoped that his
art's imitation of life would encourage his readers' lives to become imitations of art. The last words of *Tales of the Hall*
are aimed at the reader, and they hint at the possibilities
of regeneration, of "new-born feelings—Here we close/Our
Tale of Tales!—Health, reader, and repose!"

Were this the only point in the poem where the reader
seems implicated in Crabbe's autobiographical material, the
couplet would be but a whimsical, in fact a flimsy device for
concluding the whole. But the implications of the poem have
long before allied reader to character and hence to author. Alert
to Crabbe's peculiar handling of his characters, Masefield remarked that he does not remember any of them as distinct
personalities; but the long-brooding Crabbe passed "in his
brooding into ecstasy," creating figures perhaps the more haunting for being less distinct. "I do not want to know what George
the *elder brother,* was like (I fear that he was a prig), but he
speaks out of the very heart of romantic youth."[48] The disappointing priggishness of incautious George is, like the ideal
exemplariness of cautious Richard, a reflection in part of
Crabbe's ministerial role and of the decades in which he assumed its responsibilities.

Richard also speaks out of the heart of life, and Crabbe's
awareness of the universality of his highly autobiographical
Tales of the Hall is nowhere so simply revealed as in that minor
self-portrait, the sketch of the rector Jacques. Beloved by his
congregation as an individual, Jacques is mistrusted as a preacher
because the virtues he teaches are too widely applicable:

Nor was this moral minister afraid

To ask of inspiration's self the aid
Of truths by him so sturdily maintain'd,
That some confusion in the parish reign'd:
"Heathens," they said, "can tell us right from wrong,
But to a Christian higher points belong."
Yet Jacques proceeded, void of fear and shame,
In his old method, and obtain'd the name
Of *Moral Preacher*. . . .

This quotation comes from the introduction to the dialogue poem "The Natural Death of Love," eighth of the fifteen tales. This book is in all senses central to *Tales of the Hall,* and the ruthlessness with which Crabbe handles the matter of its title is surpassed in his work only in the marvelously malicious *tour de force* "Flirtation, a Dialogue," written about the same time and evidently intended for *Tales of the Hall* but suppressed and first published after his death. "The Natural Death of Love" strikes its dominant though not final note at once:

Love has slow death and sudden: wretches prove
That fate severe—the sudden death of love;
It is as if, on day serenely bright,
Came with its horrors instantaneous night;
Others there are with whom love dies away
In gradual waste and unperceived decay.
Such is that death of love that nature finds
Most fitted for the use of common minds,
The natural death. . . .

Crabbe's volumes swarm with wretches suffering that severer fate. Fortunately, Emma and Henry have known only the mercifully slower death. What has become of the romantic relationship between them will be the material of two-thirds of the poem, in which Crabbe promises

[to] try to paint
The passion failing, fading to complaint;
The gathering grief for joys remember'd yet;
The vain remonstrance, and the weak regret.

No reference is made in the poem to love that never dies

at all, so the reader, with only two choices, is forced to identify himself with Henry and Emma. And the reader truly is intended to see himself in the tale, for the symbol of love's progress becomes that of life's. This is especially clear in certain rejected lines on the inevitable migration the couple have made from love's "fairy land" to the "dark," "bleak," "cold" land of truth ("and this must be our home")—lines in which Crabbe used language reminiscent of *The Library*'s alliance of hope, joy, youth, romance, and innocence. In fairyland, Emma had remembered,

> were love's friends—hope, joy, and generous trust.
> Here are his foes—care, caution, and disgust.
> There was the warm confiding soul of youth,
> Here doubt and care, and cold assent to truth.
> Oh, 'tis beyond repair, beyond dispute,
> That flower of promise has this bitter fruit!
> Oh, 'tis a dismal fruit! I prithee strive
> For the old prospect—bid the dream revive.

Later, it is Henry who urges that they try to recapture the lost dream, and thereupon the poem reverses the common pattern of Crabbe's tales. It begins in melancholy fashion with Henry and Emma tracing in distraught retrospection the morbidly fascinating downward course their love has taken. Two prisoners in solitary confinement, they communicate only through the walls of their separate dungeons. But as the dialogue advances, growing more heated, the rather morbid satire diminishes. The appalling helplessness of the disenchanted couple gives way to a carefully phrased, humbly willed hope, so that Henry is able to announce:

> What we beheld in Love's perspective glass
> Has pass'd away—one sigh! and let it pass.
> It was a blissful vision, and it fled,
> And we must get some actual good instead:
> Of good and evil that we daily find,
> *That* we must hoard, *this* banish from the mind.

He is telling Emma that the facts must be faced and upon *them* the replica of lost love constructed. Romantic love was a castle on sand. Because the more modest replica shall be built on rock, there is hope that "though we backward look with some regret/On those first joys, we shall be happy yet." We are reminded of George, their neighbor and the narrator of their intimate dialogue. He too had paradoxically got shipwrecked upon a land of new possibilities, had then begun to see "through receding clouds the rising good." No more than he had Henry and Emma reembarked for Cythera—no, Cythera was fairyland, that "transient paradise of fools." They know they have forever "quit the blissful state,/And truth forever bars the golden gate." Explusion from this golden-gated Eden is more than a likely thing for every adult; it is obligatory. Moreover, its occurrence marks arrival at maturity, that condition in which, life being now conceived as tragic, one can begin to live. It is always painful to discover that one's paradise is an illusion, but

> The knowledge once obtain'd, the gate is barr'd;
> Or, could we enter, we should still repine,
> Unless we could the knowledge too resign.—
> Yet let us calmly view our present fate,
> And make a humbler Eden of our state;
> With this advantage, that what now we gain,
> Experience gives and prudence will retain.

Even as man's shaping and restraining powers have made of wild England a garden, Henry argues, so may expelled couples like themselves cultivate their spiritual wilderness. When the William and Frances of a later tale forgivingly reunite years after she has betrayed him, they cultivate behind the inn they run a garden which they call a "little paradise." As an affectionate couple they are now happier than they were as a passionate couple. For Henry and Emma, too, lively affection will assume the throne left vacant by dead passion; and well-considered generosities will replace selfish impulses:

> Each on the other must in all depend,
> The kind adviser, the unfailing friend;
> Through the rough world we must each other aid,
> Leading and led, obeying and obey'd;
> Favour'd and favouring, eager to believe

> What should be truth—unwilling to perceive
> What has offended, wisely to improve
> What pleases yet, and guard returning love.

This postmarital service of marriage expressly promises that truth will be discovered not to be supreme after all, nor pain and disease the inevitable plateaus to which all lives must finally sink, nor illusion and reason implacable foes.

Like his autobiographical Jacques, Crabbe uses Christian imagery for moral lessons transcending Christianity. Supposed forerunner of the Naturalists, Crabbe never denies the reality of spirit; for he sees repeated in the experience of "common minds" the archetypal pattern of fall and redemption, a pattern learned first from secular experience and observation but later confirmed by experience as priest and pronouncer of precepts. The soul prospers and withers, dies or is reborn, according to the degree to which the multitudinous passions are modified by reason; and reason eternally whispers that only humility can bring, as it brings to the elder brother George, "Health, reader, and repose!"

CHAPTER 5

Retrospections

I   *Return for a Farewell*

GEORGE Crabbe's last major poetical effort betrays a falling away of powers not unlikely in a poet entering his sixth decade of verse making. This final series of narratives, collectively entitled *Farewell and Return*, suffers also from not having been sufficiently revised. First published in 1834, two years after his death, the *Posthumous Tales* had already been lying "long undisturbed" in a recess of his Trowbridge rectory—so long undisturbed, it seems, that Crabbe forgot how much in need of revision it was. In 1831 he told his son that the stories were "fully prepared for the press."[1] With apologies for their imperfect condition, his son duly published them. But the superior pieces in *Posthumous Tales* are not those of the series but four stray ones that may well have been composed in earlier years.

The briefest of these is "Rachel," suggestive of one of those ghost tales gathered for versifying during the composition of *Tales of the Hall*. Its brevity and its first-person references to the friend who tells the tale may mean that the piece was later intended for *Farewell and Return*. Rachel is yet another of those trusting girls who become deranged after their lovers betray them, a figure Crabbe was overly fond of portraying, so much so that his fondness is itself of interest. "Rachel" is redeemed by two things: the mood paintings of the seacoast the deranged girl haunts, and the direct connection established between the depression caused by her insensitive religious advisers and the madness which the apparition of her lover precipitates. In its quick, impressionistic way, "Rachel" is a touching piece. Longer but less interesting is "The Equal Marriage," inferior to "The Preceptor Husband" (*Tales of the Hall*, IX) and "The Natural Death of Love" (*Tales of the Hall*, XIV), both of which it resembles. The death of love this tale handles is of the sudden kind; its imagery is accordingly more violent, and what replaces love is not a mordant yet constructive dialogue but a winter's tempest, and the mutually deceived, doomed couple are likened to the angler's gasping fish.

Judged by what it accomplishes, "The Family of Love" goes on too long—1,071 lines in all. Otherwise, it betrays no falling away of powers whatsoever. A leisurely piece, in which character analysis predominates over character painting and theme over action, it nevertheless captures attention early and holds it. The long-absent uncle's use of an assumed name in order to examine the true merits of relatives whom he may honor in his will is a well-worn device in literature. Crabbe had used it himself in *The Parish Register*, but here he handles it freshly. He defines, slowly and exactly, the degree to which each of the four members of the examined family falls short of his pretenses. They have all long boasted of being a "family of love," but the reader is permitted to gather such evidence as to lay each brother and sister under suspicion, until the final desperate but still unconscious self-betrayals beautifully lay all doubt aside.

The tale ends with a skillful anticlimax of a sort suggesting that it issued from impulses in Crabbe not exhausted by the composition of *Tales of the Hall*. First occurs the "conclusion" one might expect: the undeceived uncle rewards the family's unkindly neglected, never-mentioned young nephew, the only honest relative of the lot. But the poem's true point is yet to come. When the uncle announces that the outcast nephew has won the prize, he scolds his embarrassed listeners in movingly mild terms. They are creatures, he says, whose weaknesses are common rather than dreadful, regrettable rather than outrageous. Then he announces his odd but benevolent intention to blackmail them all. He may live, he says, "forgive me—years to come," so each member of the family of love shall surely have enough time to live up to the family claim; and to the degree that each does, so shall the will be altered in his favor. Crabbe's achievement at the end of this story is considerable. He leaves us convinced that the abashed family will begin to reform and that each will even come, soon, to love his examiner, judge, accuser, and forgiver. The uncle is eminently lovable, and Crabbe somehow suggests that the family will work its redemption by discovering that this is so.

The first of the four stray pieces in *Posthumous Tales* is "Silford Hall," a well-wrought poem and one of Crabbe's most beguiling. Hardly a narrative, it tells of an unspoiled, humble boy's admiring tour through a great manor and its grounds. Sent by his father on a routine and quickly managed matter of business, the impressionable boy is permitted to tour the entire estate, and so the poem's subtitle is "The Happy Day." Escorted by the housekeeper, in his eyes a grand and "ruling Lady," the boy visits the bedrooms and the chapel, the art gallery and the billiard room, the game room and the library. Once he is left alone reading in the heart of the bewildering maze and discovers, to his fright, that doors have been inadvertently locked against his escape; another time he falls asleep beneath a tree in the great park and has wild dreams. At length, this "Hero of a day" dines splendidly in the kitchen with the servants and returns home intoxicated by an experience whose details, we are told, he was still recounting in his old age. We do not need the son's note to know that the happy boy was young Crabbe, and the old man who could still remember everything about that long-lost happy day is, of course, aging Crabbe, writer of the poem. The noble seat which the boy visits belonged in actuality to the family whom Crabbe as a man was most unhappily to serve as chaplain, but the poem is virtually untouched by memories of later years.

Both "Infancy—a Fragment" (briefly examined in the first chapter) and "Silford Hall" are profoundly retrospective, looking back with nostalgia to a childlike state of innocence. But the one recollects an event which life seems mysteriously to have designed as ominous portent, whereas the other recalls an event for its own sake and all its sweetness is preserved in retrospection; in fact it is improved with age and undamaged by the bitterness of later knowledge. Crabbe deleted in manuscript a concluding section of "Silford Hall" which drew several somber moral lessons. One of them is the old two-faced argument of the second book of *The Village,* here less irritating because less querulous: the rich are not much happier than the poor, for

> Riches, and all that we desire to gain,
> Bind their possessors in a golden chain—
> 'Tis kept in peril, and 'tis lost with pain.

And the poor have, after all, something besides their "Sorrow and want," and that is British freedom. Another more interesting and more valid moral deduction lies implicit in "Silford Hall" but appears explicit in the deleted conclusion:

> Dream on, dear Boy! let pass a few brief years,
> Replete with troubles, comforts, hopes, and fears,
> Bold expectations, efforts wild and strong,
> And thou shalt find thy fond conjectures wrong.
> Imagination rules thee: thine are dreams,
> And every thing to thee is what it seems:
> Thou seest the surfaces of things, that pass
> Before thee, colour'd by thy fancy's glass.
> The fact below is hidden!

The aesthetic judgment which led Crabbe to expunge well-composed but unnecessary passages was not at work in the composition of the *Farewell and Return,* whose subject is essentially the same—the sorrowful change which time brings to nearly everyone and everything. This has, of course, always been a subject of Crabbe's work, which everywhere shows him fascinated by the simple laws of cause and effect. He ever searches beneath appearance for the hidden fact, and the fact becomes a point of departure from which he may travel through time backward to trace its cause or forward to trace its effect. This habit of mind became the very plan of his final work. Returning in mind to Aldeburgh (and sometimes, these years, in body too), Crabbe chose his own village as his setting. As we might have expected, to make his farewell he has come back to where he had begun. His task now, a reflection of his own retrospective preoccupations in these late years, is to compile a series of narratives based on the lives of friends and acquaintances to whom a man now returned to his native sea town had bid farewell twenty years before. The returning native, frankly named the Poet, is obviously Crabbe. So must be the man who brings the Poet up to date on the lives of his

friends and acquaintances—he is called simply the Friend. The
figures in the tales can hardly be unlike those in Crabbe's earlier
volumes—figures based in part upon persons Crabbe has known.

Lilian Haddakin believes that in certain lines of the fragment "Infancy," lines "though apt enough" nevertheless "con-
trived," Crabbe sought "temporary escape from feeling in the
exercise of ingenuity and in the imitations of his admired predecessor Pope."[2] An 1822 draft of the commencement of the
Farewell and Return echoes intentionally the commencement
of Pope's *Essay on Man* and half humorously invokes, as well,
Apollo, Fancy, and "whatever God or Goddess" might be of
service.[3] These are lines penned when Crabbe first conceived
the series. He could not, however, long deny his bias against
things literary which had two decades ago prompted the blunt
declaration "No Muse I ask, before my view to bring" the varied
matter of *The Parish Register;* and the opening lines of the
series as published bring us face to face with the real subjects
of the poem. No trace of conventional allusion or invocation
appears. The real subjects are, of course, such as arouse strong
feelings from which he will not permit himself to escape—
Aldeburgh, its inhabitants, himself; expectations and enchant-
ments; disenchantments and disorders.

The sea appears, too, in these uncompleted mutability cantos:
"One object only is the same; the sight/Of the wide Ocean
by the moon's pale light . . . ." Associated so often in his work
with disaster, tempestuous passions, eternal mysteries, and,
finally, himself, the sea represents the only thing that life
can promise all men, the only certainty—unceasing, unpredict-
able, and generally undesired change. This conviction controls
the simple structure of the series, dictating its juxtaposition
of drastically contrasting narrative halves separated only by the
imagined lapse of time.

As first conceived, the series was to handle its theme by surveying three things:

1. The Place itself and its Improvements
2. The Change in a Man's self—
3. That in others,—
This may be given in various Letters or in only two—the
Questions and Replies?—[4]

Occasional inconsistencies in the series as published show that
Crabbe had not fully converted his first plan (that of dividing
the entire work into two halves, one covering all farewells, the
other covering the Poet's return) into his second (that of including a farewell and a return in each separate narrative).
Besides, Crabbe fastened most of his attention on the last of
the three listed subjects, the change in others. For nearly all,
the change has been similar. Sorrowful conclusions have set
the seal of disenchantment upon bright or promising beginnings.
Love has decayed or betrayed (as in "Danvers and Rayner,"
XVIII, or "The Cousins," XXI); hopes have been blighted ("Barnaby, the Shopman," VIII); pride has fallen ("The Merchant,"
XI); religious trust in life has been shocked into religious with-
drawal from life ("Jane," IX); a pretty girl has become an ex-
asperating wife ("Belinda Waters," XV); a famous bluestocking
has sunk into oblivion because her patron died ("The Dean's
Lady," XIII). The mellowed melancholy of the aging Crabbe has
impressed itself upon these tales of the changes "in others,"
molding them as an ungentle, angry rhetoric had shaped the
craggy *Village* or as a hushed redemptive excitement had
warmed the chiller of the narratives in *Tales of the Hall.*

Only once in the published *Farewell and Return* did Crabbe
concentrate upon "The Place itself." That is in "The Ancient
Mansion" (X), a good example of Crabbe's tendency in his
last work to let recognizably genuine feeling remain incompletely
realized in language, incident, or even structure. As for "The
Change in a Man's self," a subject that might have led Crabbe
into making a survey more frankly autobiographical and retrospective than *Tales of the Hall,* he evaded the matter. When
the Friend has told his fifteen tales, each about changes in
others, and has added his own story about how an uncle secretly
rescued him from the ruin that his own folly was bringing upon
him, the Poet is expected to conclude the series by narrating his
own life history. He begs, however, to be spared the task,
glancing only and very briefly at that far-distant flight to London:

> Alas! no Uncle was my guide—my care
> Was all my own; no guardian took a share.

> I, like Columbus, for a world unknown—
> 'Twas no great effort—sacrificed my own—
> My own sad world, where I had never seen
> The earth productive, or the sky serene.

The Friend persists, for the tale has been promised, and sensational gossip will fill the vacuum if the Poet doesn't: "Let the Truth, before the Lie, be told." The Poet answers, "This might be done; but wonders I have none,/All my adventures are of Self alone." Once again the Friend urges, this time luridly suggesting that the Poet may have "lewd and wicked things to tell,/Low passions, cruel deeds, nay crimes," but the Poet takes the ringing of a dinner bell as a means of escaping the obligation, and so the *Farewell and Return* ends.

The faithful reader of Crabbe has long before acquired evidence that any adventures of Crabbe's "Self alone" have not been so trivial as the Poet pretends. He knows also where to find them. They begin to be recounted as early as *The Candidate,* when Crabbe was but a literary novice. The voice of Crabbe is still recounting them in the *Posthumous Tales,* whose self-effacing Poet, though enfeebled by age and sickness, shows that he can still resist successfully the temptation to escape from feeling. The psychic adventures of Crabbe, both pale and lurid, have always figured among the subjects of his poetry. Sometimes they have been nakedly expressed, sometimes clothed in moral abstractions; sometimes he has dissipated them in catalogs of realistic detail and sometimes distributed them among various *personae;* sometimes, and most happily, he has given them the full distancing of first-rate narrative.

Free from the accents of self-pity on the one hand and those of irascibility on the other, Crabbe's voice has throughout sustained a special sonority. It is the voice of one whose moral severity has been softened by a tenderness firmer than the humanitarian's but profounder than pity's; and it has the dignity which comes when grief and pain are given artistic shaping—such grief, too, as does not banish wit or "keep the sunshine of good humor out." Above all, it is the voice of one who, according to his own lights, was thoroughly honest.

Crabbe's lights were not always of the brightest, but his insight was such that although his poetry reflects as much of the opaque surfaces of life as does the poetry of any other English poet, it also pierces inward. Looking straight out, as he did, Crabbe so often looked nearly straight down as here and there to lay his finger quite upon the hidden pulse of life. Edwin Arlington Robinson perceived this and recorded the perception in a sonnet to the little-read Crabbe:

> Give him the darkest inch your shelf allows,
> Hide him in lonely garrets, if you will,
> But his hard human pulse is throbbing still
> With the sure strength that fearless truth endows.

II *"Fare Well" for a Return*

When Robinson identified the strength of Crabbe's poetry as lying in the fearlessness of the truths it illuminates or re-creates, he was identifying one of several ingredients that have won for Crabbe a position in English literature simultaneously significant and indefinable. Expressionistic as well as photographic, cool-headed but moody, censorious and sympathetic, Crabbe belongs as much among the post-Romantics as among the post-Augustans. Psychological and motivational, the emphases of his sketches and his narratives place him almost as surely among England's novelists as among her poets, so that we are not startled to discover Thomas Hardy saying that it was in the composition not of poetry but of prose fiction that he had gone to Crabbe for schooling.[5] Crabbe's influence on certain mannered Realists—on Hardy, Sainte-Beuve, E. A. Robinson, Pound, John Betjeman—may be defined with some precision; not so his more important influence upon certain literary movements or genres (the Victorian novel, for instance) or upon literature generally. We can safely say, however, that English literature, both prose and verse, has not been the same since the concrete language of this cleric's low-pitched couplets first effected one of those remarriages of art and life which periodically refresh a nation's literature.

A half-dozen decades have passed since Robinson wrote his sonnet to Crabbe, and the particular paradoxes of twentieth-century life have produced a climate of opinion even more favorable to Crabbe's attitudes, subjects, and technique. Heroic couplets, for one thing, have ceased to repel us; some decades ago they began to attract us again; for, in the midst of chaos, a couplet is one kind of order and a reminder of other kinds. We are somewhat less susceptible than we used to be either to the gorgeousness of much Romantic verse or to the pale purples of much Victorian. And we are less likely in this decade than we were in the two following World War I to ridicule moral emphases. Crabbe takes moral stands, but he does so in a tough-fibered way. No more than we had he a simple or comfortable view of life and its demands. Indeed, it is to the point that we now review that striking passage which Crabbe, the sexagenarian, wrote to one of the young women he was pursuing through the mails:

Self-possession is nearly but not entirely my Idea of your Character. I should say, Resignation, not only from Motives of Piety, but from Native Capacity for bearing Evil. Fitness of Mind to contend with natural and moral Adversities, the frowns of Fortune and the attacks of Malevolence.—
Did I ever tell you of a young Lady here, whom I call and who calls herself my Friend? And she might be, but she is very young and has never felt Sorrow nor left the Wing of Affection. She is of Course disposed to think, notwithstanding what old Fellows observe, that the World is a charming place and the Creatures in it good hum-oured and generous and kind and happy—and why should I, if I could [,] remove the Veil? No! perhaps it may be done by Time gently. It unfits me however for conversation.[6]

The quantity of Crabbe's output suggests that nothing had unfitted him for carrying on a dialogue of sorts with his reading public, and on these very topics—the powers of malevolence at loose in the world, the natural as well as the moral adversities, the necessity for fitness of mind, the loss of innocence. The reward for the loss of innocence, which falls away with the veils, is great: it is the high sanity which understands that the nature of things brooks no determined defiance. But Crabbe understood the loss in the gain just as well as he did the gain in the loss; nor were his battles self-regarding ones only—ones fought for himself alone. At least, his commission of them to poetry was not exhibitionistic but benedictory. We remember how the tales of tales concludes, and that hard-won benediction has peculiarly forceful impact in our own times.

It would be, therefore, both a credible thing and a hopeful sign if the present resurgence of interest in Crabbe were to make him once again a popular poet. Unlike certain once equally popular contemporaries—Southey, Samuel Rogers, Thomas Moore—Crabbe was a poet whose qualities are substantial enough to reappeal across intervening time, to transmit themselves through whatever densities of intervening school or movement. It is his fidelity to experience that has saved him for us and now makes him one of us, allows his pain to become, as he would put it, our pleasure—and our profit. The mercilessness of his psychological, scientific, and sociological probings offended the Romantics but should not strike us as strange. As psychologists, sociologists, and scientists, we have often been more cruel and less sane that was the "misanthropic" Crabbe, and his dark view is sufficiently mitigated to be constructive and affirmative in ways that ought to strike respondent chords in modern man.

Crabbe's suspicions and reservations oppose him to the post-Romantic streak of optimism we associate chiefly with Browning and H. G. Wells, and yet he seems almost cheerful and sanguine next to the Victorian pessimists one might be inclined to identify him with. His affirmations are more cautious than Carlyle's and more progessive than those of Matthew Arnold or of T. S. Eliot; all three of these have looked chiefly backward in their search for defenses against the tragic cast of life. Crabbe did not rummage the past in search of touchstones any more than he pined forward towards utopias. Both those ways romantic madness lies.

Crabbe faces the present, as must finally any man, Everyman; and in so doing he does not call in as consolation or defense mystical programs of the sort whose efficacy fades as the novelty of mysticism thins. Crabbe is positively existential, sometimes almost Existential. His "non-religious" employment of a religious myth with emphasis on personal relations[7] should be peculiarly congenial to many moderns who seek some sort of spiritual ballast for a code of ethics which a stagnant church has permitted to become unballasted. "Catastrophe conduces to contrition," wrote Marianne Moore with her eye on the recently concluded World War II. "Convictions, however, are the result of experience. Corroborated by the thinking of others —and the moral law (which is self-demonstrating, most of us admit,)—experience is almost certain to accept the fact that mystery is not just a nut which diligence can crack."[8] These words might have been composed as a brief meditation on the work of George Crabbe, who in his humble way was able to do what English poets for a century had been failing to do:[9] although he does not attempt to recreate mythological characters, he is able to revitalize a "blasted" myth and through it to talk conduct convincingly. He is actually a member of that illustrious company F. R. Leavis has identified as belonging to "the great tradition."

"Be not too hasty," Johnson's Imlac warns Rasselas, "to trust or to admire the teachers of morality: they discourse like angels, but they live like men." It is unlikely that anyone will ever accuse Crabbe of having discoursed like an angel; and, when we read the work of this poet-divine, we incline to agree with his own admission that he was able to do no more than live like a man. As sceptical as Imlac, today's reader is reassured by Crabbe's poetry that true, even great poets may speak in tongues considerably coarser than those of angels. Crabbe's poetry reassures him too that the conduct he advises is conduct it is advisable for all men to honor—and, of all men, especially us. The particular aesthetic and ethical thirsts of our mid-century lives suggest, in short, that Crabbe's return to favor ought to fare well indeed.

Notes and References

Chapter One

1. *The Poetical Works of the Rev. George Crabbe, with his Letters and Journals, and his Life, by his Son* (London, 1834), II, 84, n.
2. W. K. Thomas, "The Flavour of Crabbe," *The Dalhousie Review*, XL (Winter, 1960-61), 493.
3. Frank Whitehead, ed., *George Crabbe: Selections from His Poetry* (London, 1955), passim.
4. William Hazlitt, "Mr. Campbell.—Mr. Crabbe.," *The Spirit of the Age* (London, 1825), pp. 185-205.
5. The draft the son may have used (and taken some liberties with) covers pp. [160], [166], and [168] of MS. notebook *N* in the possession of Sir John Murray, KCVO, DSO, and is so dated.

Chapter Two

1. *Critical Review*, LVI (July, 1783), 60-61; *British Magazine and Review*, III (August, 1783), 132-34; *Gentleman's Magazine*, LIII (December, 1783), 1041-42. *Annual Register* of 1783 and *Elegant Extracts* for 1789.
2. *Life and Poems*, I, 118-19.
3. Review of 1807 *Poems, Edinburgh Review*, XII (April, 1808), 140.
4. *Life and Poems*, I, 135.
5. For an attempt to make it do so, see Rosemary Thale, "Crabbe's *Village* and Topographical Poetry," *Journal of English and Germanic Philology*, LV (October, 1956), 618-25.
6. *Life and Poems*, I, 174.
7. Letter to S. C. Hall, January 15, 1837, *The Letters of William and Dorothy Wordsworth: the Later Years*, ed. de Selincourt (Oxford, 1939), II, 829.
8. William Strang, *George Crabbe* (London, 1913), p. 33.
9. *New Poems by George Crabbe*, ed. Arthur Pollard (Liverpool, 1960), pp. 97-125. By 1826, when he wrote "Poins," Crabbe had

mellowed sufficiently to let his second thoughts replace this couplet with one less severe: "A Village then, tho' Poets may prefer/
Such Kind of Place, was not a Place for her." See Robert L.
Chamberlain, "Unpublished Poetry of Crabbe . . . with Introductory Essay," unpublished doctoral dissertation, Syracuse University, 1956, p. 225, n.

10. Paul Elmer More, "A Plea for Crabbe," *Atlantic Monthly*, LXX-
VIII (December, 1901), 857. Reprinted in *Shelburne Essays*, I.
11. Arthur Sale, ed., *The Village* (London, 1950), p. ix.
12. Precedents for Crabbe's corrective realism in handling country
life may be found in Ramsay, Churchill, Goldsmith, Somervile,
Armstrong, Dyer, Gisbourne, Graham, Duck, Jenyns, Prior, and
others. See, for example, Oliver Elton, *Survey of English Literature, 1739-1780* (New York, 1928), II, 348; Harold Mantz,
"Non-dramatic Pastoral in Europe in the Eighteenth Century,"
Publications of the Modern Language Association, XXXI (1916),
442-43; J. W. Draper, "The Metrical Tale in XVIII-Century
England," *Publications of the Modern Language Association*,
LII (1937), 390-97; Varley Lang, "Crabbe and the Eighteenth
Century," *English Literary History*, V (1938), 304-33; Sale,
ed., *The Village*, passim.
13. Review of 1807 *Poems, Anti-Jacobin Review*, XXVIII (December, 1807), 340.
14. F. R. Leavis, *Revaluation* (London, 1949), p. 128.
15. Thale, p. 623; Meyer Howard Abrams, *The Mirror and the
Lamp* (New York, 1953), p. 52.
16. Hoxie N. Fairchild, *The Noble Savage* (New York, 1928), p.
302.
17. Crabbe began *The Library* at least as early as June, 1779. In
a 1779 MS notebook owned by Sir John Murray, an early
draft of the poem, already entitled (in cypher) *Library*, is
broken a third of the way through by the notation "I wrote this/
6.30." He took the poem with him to London in April, 1780,
and may have reworked it several times before publishing it.
18. Lilian Haddakin, *The Poetry of Crabbe* (London, 1954), p. 76.
19. MS notebook [*Poet's Journal*], Murray Collection, pp. [47]-[90].
20. *George Crabbe*, p. 24.
21. Robert L. Chamberlain, "George Crabbe and Darwin's Amorous
Plants," *Journal of English and Germanic Philology*, LXI (October, 1962), 833-52.
22. In an earlier MS draft, the longer treatment of the ingredients
of romance evokes chiefly *The Faerie Queene*, including even
Acrasia's beguiling but sinister bower: "Alas no more I see My

Queen repair/To balmy Bower[s] that blossom in the Air/ Where on th[ei]r rosy Beds the Graces rest,/And hope a[nd] joy lie panting on the Breast." Later, Crabbe condensed and generalized, apparently in order to suggest various types of romantic literature—epic, medieval romance, Gothic novel, and folktale.

23. Letter from Crabbe to Burke, June 26, 1781, in *The Correspondence of Sir Th. Hanmer* (London, 1838), p. 385. This letter is reprinted in René Huchon, *George Crabbe and his Times: 1754-1832*, trans. Frederick Clarke (London, 1907), pp. 493-98.

24. Strang, p. 8.

Chapter Three

1. Letter from Scott to Lady Abercorn, August 2, 1820, in *Familiar Letters of Sir Walter Scott*, ed. D. D. (Edinburgh, 1894), II, 94; review of *Poems, Quarterly Review*, IV (November, 1810), 294.

2. For a difference of opinion regarding the effect of opium upon Crabbe's poetry, compare Meyer Howard Abrams, *The Milk of Paradise* (Cambridge, Mass., 1934) and Elisabeth Schneider, *Coleridge, Opium, and Kubla Khan* (Chicago, 1953).

3. I have given a more detailed treatment of the subjects on this page and the following several in "George Crabbe and Darwin's Amorous Plants."

4. Norton Garfinkle, "Science and Religion in England, 1790-1800," *Journal of the History of Ideas*, XVI (June, 1955), 376-88.

5. Reviews of *The Borough, Monthly Review*, LXI (April, 1810), 398-99, and in *Eclectic Review*, VI (April, 1810), 549-57.

6. *The Captain's Death Bed* (New York, 1950), p. 31.

7. Patrick Cruttwell, "The Last Augustan," *Hudson Review*, VII (Winter, 1954), 541; Geoffrey Grigson, ed., *Selected Poems of George Crabbe* (London, 1951), pp. 7-8.

8. See Philarète Chasles, "De la Poésie Chartiste en Angleterre," *Revue des Deux Mondes*, LX (1845), 326-39, and L. Etienne, "Les Poètes des pauvres en Angleterre" *Revue des Deux Mondes*, V, n.s., (1856), 370-400.

9. Arthur Sale, "Chaucer in Cancer," *English*, VI, 35 (Summer, 1947), 240-44. Comparing Jachin's tale in *The Borough* and Chaucer's Pardoner's Tale, Sale concluded that "Out of his surplice, Parson Crabbe is not so much unlike Chaucer—raised forefinger and all."

10. Review of *Poems, Edinburgh Review*, XII (April, 1808), 132.

11. J. G. Lockhart, *Memoirs of Sir Walter Scott* (London, 1900), V, 423; Thomas, "Flavour of Crabbe," p. 493.

12. Queries posed in Whitehead's notes to the *Register* in his *Selections* lead the reader to appreciate the relationship between the texture of Crabbe's language and his skill in character drawing. Haddakin's *Poetry of Crabbe* also contains explications of this sort, for example, pp. 75-80 and 137-40.

13. Review of *Poems, Gentleman's Magazine,* LXXVII (November, 1807), 1038.

14. Whitehead, p. 158, n. to 11. 59-66.

15. A. C. Hillier, "Jane Austen's Husband," *Temple Bar,* CXII (November, 1897), 352.

16. *Eclectic Review,* VI, 40-42.

17. P. 141.

18. E. M. Forster, "George Crabbe," *Spectator,* CXLVII (February, 1932), 243-45.

19. P. 398.

20. More, "A Plea for Crabbe," pp. 854-55.

21. Letters to Lawrence Binyon and Iris Barry, *The Letters of Ezra Pound,* ed. D. D. Paige (London, 1951), pp. 403, 140.

22. *Alfred Lord Tennyson: a Memoir by his Son* (London, 1897), II, 287; C. H. Herford, *English Tales in Verse* (London, 1902), p. 50.

23. F. A. Pottle, "Preface" to Margaret Ashmun's *The Singing Swan: An Account of Anna Seward* (New Haven, 1931), p. ix.

24. Wallace Cable Brown, "Crabbe: Neo-Classic Narrative," *The Triumph of Form* (Chapel Hill, N. C., 1948), p. 188ff.

25. Oliver Elton, "The Poetry of Crabbe," *Blackwood's Magazine,* CLXXXV (January, 1909), 82.

26. *Revaluation,* p. 126.

27. "George Crabbe," p. 244.

28. Review of *The Borough, Quarterly Review,* IV (November, 1810), 282.

29. *Life and Poems,* I, 165.

30. "Flavour of Crabbe," p. 492.

31. *Quarterly Review,* IV, 306.

32. "The England of George Crabbe," *Social Studies in English Literature* (New York, 1916), p. 94.

Chapter Four

1. Letter from Lockhart to his wife, August, 1825, *Family Letters of Scott,* II, 343.

2. Chapter XIV of *Biographia Literaria.*

3. See Walter Broman, "Factors in Crabbe's Eminence in the Early Nineteenth Century," *Modern Philology*, LI (August, 1953), 42-49.
4. *Autobiography of Mrs. Fletcher* (Edinburgh, 1875), p. 154; René Huchon, "A Brief Appreciation of the Crabbe Collection at Bath" (September, 1905), a pamphlet; Huchon, *George Crabbe*, pp. 250-51.
5. *Les Générations Littéraries* (Paris, 1948), p. 130.
6. Crabbe's fondness for *Night Thoughts* may have led him to an imitation, the rather un-Crabbean "Midnight." The proof that this poem is Crabbe's remains limited—see Adolphus Ward, ed., *Poems by George Crabbe* (Cambridge, 1905-07), I, viii.
7. Lucas, "A Poet of Prose," *Life and Letters*, VI, 33 (February, 1931), 100; Grigson, "Introduction," *Selected Poems of George Crabbe* (London, 1951), p. 7.
8. [Francis Hodgson,] *Childe Harold's Monitor*, quoted in *Gentleman's Magazine*, LXXXVIII, ii (August, 1818), 138.
9. Chamberlain, "Unpublished Poetry," pp. lxvii-lxix; Elton, "The Poetry of Crabbe," p. 79.
10. See Chamberlain, "George Crabbe and Darwin's Amorous Plants," *passim*.
11. *Spirit of the Age*, I, 122-23.
12. P. W. Clayden, ed., *Rogers and his Contemporaries* (London, 1889), pp. 49-50.
13. *Table Talk and Omnia* (Oxford, 1917), pp. 293-94.
14. Undated letter in Lockhart, *Memoirs of Scott*, II, 241-42.
15. Broman, "Factors in Crabbe's Eminence," p. 44; Elton, "The Poetry of Crabbe," p. 79.
16. "Poins" in *New Poems by Crabbe*, p. 117.
17. *Selections*, p. 197, n. for 11. 158-69.
18. Cruttwell, p. 539.
19. Basil Willey, *The Seventeenth Century Background* (New York, 1950), p. 294.
20. *Common Sense: a Poem* (Edinburgh, 1819), pp. 15-17.
21. *Life and Poems*, I, 322.
22. Morse Peckham, "Toward a Theory of Romanticism," *Publications of the Modern Language Association*, LXVI (March, 1951), 10.
23. "Crabbe and Grimes," p. 181.
24. T. E. Welby, *Second Impressions* (London, 1933), p. 125; W. H. Hutton, "Some Memories of George Crabbe," *Burford Papers* (London, 1905), pp. 291-92.
25. "Theory of Romanticism," p. 16.

26. Hermann Hesse, *Demian,* translator not named (New York, 1948), p. 2.
27. Richard Jefferies, *The Story of My Heart* (London, 1947), p. 79.
28. George Santayana, "Lucretius," *Three Philosophical Poets* (New York, 1953), p. 47.
29. *Selections,* p. 25.
30. Review of *Tales, Edinburgh Review,* XX (November, 1812), 289.
31. Arthur Sale, "The Development of Crabbe's Narrative Art," *The Cambridge Journal,* V, 8 (May, 1952), 492-93.
32. Helen Gardner, "Milton's 'Satan' and the Theme of Damnation in Elizabethan Tragedy," *English Studies,* I (1948), 47.
33. *Life and Poems,* V, 163, n.
34. John Masefield, "George Crabbe," *Recent Prose* (London, 1932), p. 320.
35. Letter to Elizabeth Charter, July 18, 1816, in Broadley and Jerrold, eds., *The Romance of an Elderly Poet* (London, 1913), p. 139.
36. Chamberlain, "Unpublished Poetry," p. 40.
37. *Edinburgh Review,* XXXII (July, 1819), 125.
38. Huchon, *George Crabbe,* p. 406.
39. In a rough draft of *Childe Harold,* the Childe's last name appears as *Burun,* an ancestral form of *Byron*—see Moore's *Life* (London, 1860), p. 151. As we shall see, it is no coincidence, either, that a central figure in *Tales of the Hall* is named George.
40. *Life and Poems,* I, 217-18.
41. Letter to Elizabeth Charter, August 23, 1815 in *Romance of an Elderly Poet,* p. 103.
42. Letter to Elizabeth Charter, November 25, 1815; *ibid.,* p. 115.
43. Letter to Elizabeth Charter, August 25, 1819; *ibid.,* p. 253.
44. Letter to Elizabeth Charter, November 24, 1815; *ibid.,* p. 116.
45. Letter to Elizabeth Charter, January 2, 1816; *ibid.,* p. 126.
46. "Art and Neurosis" [1945], *The Liberal Imagination* (New York, 1953), pp. 173, 177.
47. *The Idea of a University* (New York, 1947), p. 132.
48. *Recent Prose,* pp. 319-20.

Chapter Five

1. *Life and Poems,* VIII, vii, v. See also Huchon, *George Crabbe,* p. 440.
2. *Poetry of Crabbe,* p. 39.
3. Chamberlain, "Unpublished Poetry," pp. cxlvii, 152-53.
4. *New Poems,* p. 175.

5. Clement Shorter, "To the Immortal Memory of George Crabbe," *Immortal Memories* (London, 1907), pp. 126-27; but see also letter from Florence Hardy to Sydney Cockerell, February 6, 1918, *Friends of a Lifetime* . . . (London, 1940), pp. 300-01.

6. Letter to Elizabeth Charter, January 2, 1816, *Romance of an Elderly Poet*, p. 126.

7. As the rest of my sentence might indicate, I employ the word *non-religious* as an allusion to *Honest to God*, John Robinson's popularization of certain contemporary theological trends.

8. "Religion and the Intellectuals: a Symposium," *Partisan Review,* XVII, 2 (February, 1950), 137.

9. Willey, *Seventeenth Century Background*, pp. 296-97.

Selected Bibliography

PRIMARY SOURCES

The most complete edition of Crabbe's poems was edited in three
volumes by Adolphus Ward for the Cambridge English Classics:
Poems by George Crabbe (Cambridge: Cambridge University Press,
1905-07). Less complete but useful as a one-volume edition is A. J.
and R. M. Carlyle's *The Poetical Works of George Crabbe* (Oxford: Oxford University Press, 1914). About half the poetry in the
Murray MS collection of Crabbe has recently appeared in *New
Poems by George Crabbe,* ed. Arthur Pollard (Liverpool: Gregory
Lounz, 1960)—poems inferior to Crabbe's other work. A few poems
published in periodicals remain uncollected. The most interesting of
editions is that edited by Crabbe's son: *The Poetical Works of the
Rev. George Crabbe: with his Letters and Journals, and his Life,
by his Son* (London: John Murray, 1834), 8 vols. In this edition
appear for the first time the *Posthumous Tales,* as large a quantity
of unrelated poems, the attractive biography, and informative notes.
The best collected edition of Crabbe published during his lifetime
is the one he himself edited for Murray in 1822 (7 volumes), reprinted in 1823 (in 5 volumes, then in 8 volumes).

Useful to the reader who wishes immediate introduction to
Crabbe's best work are a number of twentieth-century selections of
his verse (see "Criticism of Crabbe's Poetry," below), but few are
readily available in the United States. The titles and publication
dates of the first editions of Crabbe's separate poems may be found
under "Chronology."

Of his prose publications, mention need be made only of a short
autobiographical essay first published in *The New Monthly Magazine,* IV (January, 1816), pp. 511-17, reprinted in the British Museum's *Memoirs of Eminent Persons;* and *Posthumous Sermons*
(London: John Hastings, 1850).

SECONDARY SOURCES

1. Crabbe's Life

The first full-scale life of Crabbe, begun by his son George a few

years before his father's death, was published two years after it in
1834 (see above). The definitive biography, written by a Frenchman,
did not appear until the next century: René Huchon, *George Crabbe
and His Times 1754-1832*, trans. Frederick Clarke (London: John
Murray, 1907). If neither of these biographies is available, the student might turn to Thomas Kebbel's *Life of George Crabbe* (London:
Walter Scott, 1888) or, better, the *Crabbe* which Alfred Ainger
published fifteen years later in the English Men of Letters Series.

The Leadbeater Papers (London: Bell and Daldy, 1862), Vol.
II, contains letters exchanged between Crabbe and a female Irish
writer who initiated the correspondence out of admiration for his
poetry. Nearly half the letters were written between December, 1816,
and the publication of *Tales of the Hall* in 1819. Of more varied
interest is the material published by A. M. Broadley and W. Jerrold
in *The Romance of an Elderly Poet* (London: Paul, 1913). Half
this volume consists of letters, chiefly to Elizabeth Charter, written
by Crabbe between 1815 and 1825; the other half consists of the
editors' amiable running commentary, chiefly biographical. A generous handful of other letters by Crabbe has been published in volumes devoted to other figures.

2. Criticism of Crabbe's Poetry

Besides the items listed in the separate entries below and others
referred to in the footnotes, the interested reader might consult
the relevant pages in various literary histories: for example, George
Saintsbury, *History of Nineteenth Century Literature* (London: Mac-
millan, 1896), pp. 1-3, 7-9, or Harold Child, *Cambridge History of
English Literature*, XI, 140-52; but the best such is Sir J. J. C. Grierson and J. C. Smith, *A Critical History of English Poetry* (London:
Chatto and Windus, 1944), pp. 246-62.

In selections of Crabbe's poetry and editions of the son's *Life*
appear helpful introductory essays by various hands—Sir Arthur
Quiller-Couch's in *George Crabbe: Selections* (Oxford: Clarendon,
1908), A. C. Deane's in *Selections from Crabbe* (London: Methuen,
1932), F. L. Lucas' in *George Crabbe: an Anthology* (Cambridge, England: Cambridge University Press, 1933), Philip Henderson's in *George Crabbe: Poems* (London: Lawson and Dunn, 1946),
Geoffrey Grigson's in *Selected Poems of George Crabbe* (London:
Grey Walls Press, 1951), Frank Whitehead's in *George Crabbe: Selections from His Poetry* (London: Chatto and Windus, 1955), E. M.
Forster's in his edition of the *Life* (London: Oxford University Press,
1932), and Edmund Blunden's in another edition of the *Life* (London: Cresset Press, 1947). For the best of these, see Forster, Lucas,
and Whitehead, below.

Anyone concerned with Crabbe's treatment by his contemporaries should first of all consult the journals of the time—see Huchon, *George Crabbe,* pp. 523-25, for bibliographical help. Huchon's book contains by far the longest bibliography for Crabbe (pp. 518-30), but it comes up only to 1906 and is not exhaustive for the nineteenth century.

The following list is a further selection of titles most likely to be of interest or of use to the reader of Crabbe:

Brett, Raymond L. *Crabbe.* London: Longmans, 1956. A long essay attempting to rebut the more common objections to Crabbe's poetry from Hazlitt on. 43 pp.

Broman, Walter. "Factors in Crabbe's Eminence in the Early Nineteenth Century," *Modern Philology,* LI (August, 1953), 42-49. Uses Crabbe's popularity among early nineteenth-century readers as a way of identifying Romantic strains in his verse.

Brown, Wallace Cable. "Crabbe: Neo-Classic Narrative," *The Triumph of Form: a Study of the Later Masters of the Heroic Couplet.* Chapel Hill: University of North Carolina Press, 1948. A good introduction to Crabbe's versification but equally concerned with illustrating Crabbe's skill in handling narrative, dialogue, and psychological analysis.

Chamberlain, Robert L. "George Crabbe and Darwin's Amorous Plants," *Journal of English and Germanic Philology* LXI (October, 1962), 833-52. Investigates Crabbe's awareness of Erasmus Darwin's declining reputation as a way of estimating the degree to which Crabbe responded to the narrowing temper of the years 1783-1807.

Cruttwell, Patrick. "The Last Augustan," *Hudson Review,* VII (1954), 533-54. An admiring, provocative study; presents Crabbe as a man of turbulent feelings and his poetry as, therefore, caught uneasily between the demands of Neoclassical decorum (reinforced by contemporary prudishness) and Crabbe's natural impulses towards frankness (reinforced by the new Realism).

Elton, Oliver. "The Poetry of Crabbe," *Blackwood's Magazine,* CLXXXV (January, 1909), 78-90. Presents Crabbe as simply a predecessor of the Romantic movement, not a prophet of it. Yet his poetry is a refreshing antidote to the "Alastors" of literature; and, if he ever does have his long-delayed day, it will be a lasting one.

Fitzgerald, Edward. "Crabbe's *Tales of the Hall," Works of Edward Fitzgerald.* New York: Houghton Mifflin, 1887. Vol I. Appendix to "Suffolk Sea Phrases," *Ibid.,* II. Neither of these is actually as stimulating (or as trustworthy) as the references to Crabbe scattered through Fitzgerald's letters. Fitzgerald was Crabbe's most devoted nineteenth-century reader, but his heavily edited condensation of *Tales of the Hall* is of dubious value.

Forster, E. M. "George Crabbe," *Spectator*, CXLVII (February, 1932), 243-45.

——. "Introduction." *The Life of George Crabbe by his Son.* London: Oxford University Press, 1932.

——. "George Crabbe: the Poet and the Man," *Peter Grimes*: *Essays by Benjamin Britten, E. M. Forster, Montague Slater, Edward Sackville-West.* London: John Lane, 1946.

——. "George Crabbe and Peter Grimes," *Two Cheers for Democracy.* London: Edward Arnold, 1951. The fourth of these four pieces is the most substantial and valuable, informed by Forster's usual sensitivity and shrewdness; the third, having been first written about this very English poet during wartime, is the most unguardedly affectionate.

Gilfillan, George. "George Crabbe," *A Second Gallery of Literary Portraits.* Edinburgh: James Hogg, 1850. Of historical interest as an appreciation by a leader of the extravagant Spasmodics.

Gregor, Ian. "The Last Augustan," *Dublin Review,* CLXXIX (First Quarter, 1955), 37-50. Illustrates in several ways the limited "kind of deflexion that Crabbe's poetry made from the Augustan norm"—*The Village* blends colors freshly but is traditional "elegiac pastoral"; the "bizarre strength" of Crabbe's realism comes simply from his being a regionalist; his morality is subtly projected but orthodox.

Haddakin, Lilian F. *The Poetry of Crabbe.* London: Chatto and Windus, 1954. So far, the only book-length attempt to define the peculiar achievement of Crabbe, and perhaps the most successful so far. Miss Haddakin emphasizes the relationships between Crabbe's technique, the raw materials of his poetry, and the finished product—representative chapter titles are "The Experiencing Mind," "Order," and " 'Why not in Prose?' " 176 pp.

Hazlitt, William. "Mr. Campbell.—Mr. Crabbe," *The Spirit of the Age.* London: H. Colburn, 1825. Portion on Crabbe reprinted with variations from *London Magazine* (1821). Dazzling rhetoric but misleading criticism; an influence upon almost all unfavorable criticism of Crabbe thereafter. Hazlitt draws an exaggeratedly dark, unwholesome picture of the world of Crabbe's poetry and, incidentally, of the mind of its composer. His superbly Romantic reaction to Crabbe includes a troubling degree of awe.

Ker, W. P. "George Crabbe," *On Modern Literature: Lectures and Addresses.* Oxford: Clarendon Press, 1955. Crabbe's subject matter and style are not what popular opinion says, disgusting and unpoetic; they are, rather, "admirable for narrative poetry," and Crabbe himself is essentially good humored, "a chronicler of human life without any prejudice in favour of misery."

Lang, Varley. "Crabbe and the Eighteenth Century," *English Literary History,* V (March, 1938), 305-33. Valuable essay. Labels and examines the Augustan characteristics of Crabbe's thought and verse; groups them under the headings pastoral, satire, Humanism, and Neoclassic theory.

Leavis, F. R. *Revaluation.* London: Chatto and Windus, 1949. Pages 124-29 are studded with suggestive remarks on Crabbe as an Augustan artist and his verse as "a living classic."

Looker, Samuel. "In Praise of Crabbe," *19th Century,* CX (October, 1931), 489-502. Crabbe's real strength lies in his psychological insight, in his "profound knowledge of human character and his mastery and understanding of the tragi-comedy of life in a wide sense." Especially admires *Tales of the Hall.*

Lucas, F. L. "The Poet of Prose," *Life and Letters,* VI (February, 1931), 79-105. Reprinted in 1933 as introduction to a selection of Crabbe's poems. A graceful essay on the thesis that Crabbe's several deficiencies—in taste and technique—are less important than his virtues. His is poetry that surely will endure.

Masefield, John. "George Crabbe," *Recent Prose.* London: William Heinemann, 1932. A narrative poet's revaluation of a quite different sort of narrative poet. Masefield had long "either disliked or shrunk from" Crabbe's works, but he has recently been lead to reread him and "be more just."

More, Paul Elmer. "A Plea for Crabbe," *Atlantic Monthly,* LXXXVIII (December, 1901), 850-57. Reprinted in *Shelburne Essays,* I. A neo-Humanist's legitimately appreciative but overstated defense of the ethical, anti-Romantic Crabbe. More finds it no surprise that readers demanding "the rapturous liberties of Shelley and Keats" are repelled by Crabbe's "clean, good sense."

Pound, Ezra. *ABC of Reading.* London: Routledge, 1934.

———. *The Letters of Ezra Pound.* Ed. D. D. Paige. London: Faber and Faber, 1951.

———. *The Literary Essays of Ezra Pound.* London: Faber and Faber, 1954. Pound awards, *passim,* high praise to Crabbe, who differs from the usual nineteenth-century poet in not being a boring "idiot who occasionally makes beautiful (or ornamental) verses."

Sale, Arthur. "Chaucer in Cancer," *English*, VI, 35 (Summer, 1947), 240-44.

——. Introduction and notes to *The Village*. London: University Tutorial Press, 1950.

——. "The Development of Crabbe's Narrative Art," *The Cambridge Journal*, V (May, 1952), 480-98. The 1947 article finds Crabbe a modified Chaucer, and the edition of *The Village* contains much information about Crabbe's eighteenth-century predecessors. The 1952 article is the most important short study of Crabbe in this century. By tracing changing aspects of Crabbe's technique from the *Register* through the 1812 *Tales*, Sale defines Crabbe's true and considerable dimensions as a narrative poet.

Smith, Horace, and James Smith. *Rejected Addresses*. London: J. Miller, 1812. Often reprinted since. Every student of Crabbe should read this parody, the best in the volume, but then read a few poems in Alexander Balfour's *Characters Omitted in Crabbe's Parish Register* (Edinburgh: Constable, 1825) to see that Crabbe cannot really be imitated.

Stephen, Leslie. "Crabbe's Poetry," *Hours in a Library*. 2nd series. London: Smith, Elder, and Co., 1881. First published in *Cornhill Magazine*, 1874. In Woodberry's words, a "good-humored but unsuccessful attempt to appreciate Crabbe." Essentially out of sympathy with the "true poet" he undertook to promote, Stephen nevertheless did make a number of sound, stimulating observations about Crabbe.

Strang, William. *George Crabbe*. London: University College, 1913. A concise readable survey of Crabbe's life and major poems, affectionate and usually trustworthy. Defends Crabbe from Hazlitt by allying him to Chaucer. 123 pp.

Thomas, Edward. "George Crabbe," *A Literary Pilgrim in England* London: Methuen, 1917. Emphasizes effect of Aldeburgh upon Crabbe's temperament and claims that, although Crabbe's subjectivity may be a logical defect, it is certainly a poetic strength.

Thomas, W. K. "The Flavour of Crabbe," *The Dalhousie Review*, XL (Winter, 1960-61), 489-504. Interesting survey of aspects of Crabbe's verse—his use of nature description, his preference for types, and his dependence upon moral norms—which identify him as an Augustan and yet have kept his work from seriously dating.

Whitehead, Frank, ed. *George Crabbe: Selections from His Poetry*. London: Chatto and Windus, 1955. The excellent twenty-page introduction and the forty-five pages of notes and queries present Crabbe as a major English poet and constitute a first-rate piece of criticism.

Woodberry, George Edward. "Crabbe," *Studies in Letters and Life*. New York; Houghton Mifflin, 1890. First published as "A Neglected Poet," *Atlantic Monthly* (1880). Crabbe is a thoroughly honest realist of much more than historical importance, although his "almost perfect physical vision" placed limitations upon his art, keeping it at a level beneath that of Wordsworth, Shelley, or Burns.

Wylie, Laura J. "The England of George Crabbe," *Social Studies in English Literature*. New York: Houghton Mifflin, 1916. Crabbe's firsthand experience with lower-class life makes him "the spokesman of the workaday men and women of England in his time," and his studies of their character and lot "infinitely widen our knowledge of human life and our sympathy with it."

Index